Celebration of Grace

A Francis Asbury Press Book

Celebration
of
Grace

Living in Freedom

Joseph R. Cooke

Formerly published as
Free for the Taking

ZondervanPublishingHouse
Academic andProfessionalBooks
Grand Rapids, Michigan

A Division of HarperCollins*Publishers*

Celebration of Grace
Copyright © 1991 by Joseph R. Cooke

Requests for information should be addressed to:
Zondervan Publishing House
Academic and Professional Books
1415 Lake Drive S.E.
Grand Rapids, Michigan 49506

Library of Congress Cataloging-in-Publication Data

Cooke, Joseph R.
    [Free for the taking]
    Celebration of grace : living in freedom / Joseph R. Cooke.
       p.   cm.
    Reprint. Originally published: Free for the taking. Old Tappan,
N.J. : F.H. Revell Co., 1975.
    ISBN 0-310-52961-1
    1. Grace (Theology)   I. Title.
    [BT761.2.C64 1990]
    234'.1–dc20   90-44748
                                                   CIP

Printed in the United States of America

91 92 93 94 95 96 / AK / 10 9 8 7 6 5 4 3 2 1

This edition is printed on acid-free paper and meets the American
National Standards Institute Z39.49 standard.

TABLE OF CONTENTS

PREFACE TO THIS EDITION

This book is a new edition of an earlier book first published in 1975 under the title *Free for the Taking: The Life-Changing Power of Grace*. This new edition is essentially the same as the old, with a few editorial changes and, of course, a new title. I should explain, however, that the book is not strictly a book *about* celebration. It is simply a book about grace—God's love that meets us where we are, not where we ought to be. And this grace, this love, is by its very nature something to celebrate with heartfelt joy and thanksgiving. Indeed, it is God's own Good News, and as such it is worthy of being received, enjoyed, and celebrated, not only now but throughout eternity.

I should explain, too, that the primary focus here is grace for the struggling saint rather than for the lost sinner (though I have heard of unbelievers coming to Christ through reading it). In a general sense, then, the book is for Christians who want to understand and live out the Gospel of Grace more fully in their minds and hearts, in their feelings and decisions, and in relationships with God and others.

In a special sense, however, it's for believers who are living burdened, squirrel-cage lives, earnestly trying to please a God who is almost impossible to please. It's also for Christian workers (missionaries, pastors, and others) who are involved in high-commitment ministries that place a high premium on modeling Christian life and service; for such worthy servants of God often feel themselves almost forced to live beyond their spiritual means. Therefore, they sometimes face intense nongrace pressures. Finally, it is for those involved in some kind of Christian counseling ministry, who need something to pass on to those who seek their help.

In short, the book is intended to meet very real needs that God's people often have to deal with. Indeed, ever since it went out of print, I have continued to hear from people who wanted to have the book for themselves or who needed it for their counseling ministry. I am therefore thankful to see it in print again. I hope that God will keep on using it to bring His children out of spiritual slavery and into the freedom, joy, and fruitfulness that God intends for all of us. I know that this *can* be a freeing, life-changing book, for I have met those who have told me so out of their own experiences. So if the reader should indeed be hungry for such change, I pray that he or she will find something here that meets this need—something that enables him or her to enter into a life of the celebration of grace.

Also, as I release this book for the second time, I would like again to express my appreciation to my dear wife, Laura, now with the Lord. She stood with me through all the years of struggle that went into my search for a deeper understanding of grace; and she walked faithfully with me through the long, painful stretches of time when our marriage was anything but sweet—including some pretty difficult years that we faced even after I wrote glowingly (in the Preface to the first edition) of the joys of our then-transformed relationship.

I do want to say, further, that in the three or four years before Laura passed away, we both expended a great deal of time and effort dealing with some of the previously obscure but unfinished business between us. And we found ourselves learning to be much more realistic, open, sharing, and forgiving toward each other than we had ever been before.

Ironically, it was just as Laura was really opening herself up in a new way to life, to me, to friends, and to God that she came down with Lou Gehrig's disease (or ALS, as medical people call it). She responded to this new test with incredible courage, holding indomitably to her love for me, for her many friends, and for God. As I sought to stand by her—as she once had stood by me—I found myself watching as, week by week, month by month, she slowly lost the use of her body—her ability to play the piano, to walk, to use her hands, to write, to swallow, to speak, and finally even to breathe. In fact at the end her body had become a prison that locked her mind, fully aware but silent, within a world of almost total impotence. She could scarcely even make known her most basic needs except by moving her eyes in response to yes/no questions. But then on August 2, 1990, God, in His infinite mercy, called her home.

Needless to say, we shed many tears together during the last months of her illness. And now, for me, the tears still fall from time to time as I walk on alone, with no Laura by my side. But she—she is free now. She has met her Lord face to face and at this very moment is experiencing joys beyond all imagining—joys that I can only wait for. Indeed, she now knows far better than I what the celebration of grace really means. And I cannot wish it otherwise.

To her, then, I dedicate this second edition.

Joseph R. Cooke
August 1990

PREFACE TO THE FIRST EDITION

The reader may have gathered from the title of this book that the following pages are all about grace. But really this is a book about love, for grace is nothing more or less than the face that love wears when it meets imperfection, weakness, failure, sin. Grace is what love is and does when it meets the sinful and the undeserving. It's what enables us to see beyond one another's faults so that we can love one another without reference to whether that love has been earned or deserved. It's what God does when He reaches out in love for us—sinful as we are—and welcomes us into a relationship with Himself.

In fact God's love for us is always grace-colored. Every loving thought and action of God toward us is necessarily an expression of grace. For we are never worthy of the least of the loving kindnesses He keeps pouring out upon us. Nothing that He does for us or gives to us is ever merited. Rather, His is a love that reaches out to us eternally, without stint, and beyond all deserving. It is pure gift. And it's ours, free for the taking. That's what grace is.

I hope, then, that the following pages will give the reader a clear picture of what grace is, that it is not just a matter of intellectual understanding but a day-by-day experience. For grace is not merely something to be understood; it's something to be lived. I hope, too, that the reader will come to know the God of grace in a new and vital way; for in the final analysis, all grace comes from Him.

I wish to express my heartfelt appreciation to all who have made this book possible: the people who have listened to my talks on grace; the people who have urged me to put my thoughts into print; those who have read parts of what I have written and made helpful suggestions; and above all my wife.

It will become obvious to the reader that my wife and I have been through some bitter times together—times when each of us made the grace life all but unattainable for the other. But there has been another side to the picture. For the past several years, God has been doing something special for us, and our whole relationship has been transformed.

This book is one of the by-products of our experience with God. For years I had tried to write down some of the thoughts God had given me on the subject of grace, but always with meager results. It took a renewed relationship with my wife to bring my efforts to fruition—that, and her interest, encouragement, and help. For these and her many suggestions, I thank her with all my heart.

J.R.C.

INTRODUCTION

There was a day for me when my whole life caved in—
when the edifice that I had painstakingly erected over many
years came tumbling down like a house of cards. I had been
born into a Christian home, carefully nurtured in Christian
schools, surrounded by a Christian environment, and enriched by many Christian teachers and friends. I had early
made a confession of Christ, and had grown year by year in
Christian knowledge and teaching. I had also committed my
life to Christ, received excellent Christian training in a good
Bible college, and been commissioned as a missionary to
Thailand under a reputable Christian mission board. Life had
seemed wonderful. In so far as I was able, I had gone all the
way with Christ, and I was looking forward to the
challenges and rewards of a lifetime of missionary service.

And yet . . . after three years as a missionary in
Thailand, I found myself at the end of the road. I had what
they call a nervous breakdown, and became totally unable to
go on. Instead, I had to return to the United States with my
tail between my legs, so to speak. All my hopes and
aspirations were shattered, and all the skills that I had
acquired through the years of preparation became unusable.
For I soon found myself unable to preach, unable to teach,
unable to read my Bible, unable to pray, unable to face the
least spiritual challenge or duty without the threat of
personal disintegration. I was of no use to God, to my wife,
to myself, to anyone. I had been reduced to absolute zero,
and somehow I had to find a way to put my life back
together and learn to live all over again.

This is not the place to tell about the long, slow climb
back to life, hope, and wholeness; but I do want to tell you

about one thing that has been crucial in this process—a new understanding and appreciation of the grace of God.

Not that I was entirely ignorant of the grace of God before. I had always believed it and prized it as a central part of my faith. I had carefully studied Paul's teachings on the subject, especially as developed in the book of Romans and in Galatians; and I had frequently preached and taught these same truths. But at the same time, on a deeper level, I had lived most of my life with a legalistic, ungracious God. Only as I began to see how profoundly I had been living under the shadow of such a God, and to see the meaning of His grace on the heart-habit level, was I able to begin to work my way through to a life of greater freedom and fulfillment. Because of these experiences, I want to share some of the things I have learned so that other Christians may avoid these same pitfalls and find a new and fruitful way to live.

1 | LIVING WITH THE PERFORMANCE GAP

THE LAW OF GOD: WHAT IT IS

It is difficult to write about the grace of God without considering God's law. Those who fail to take the law of God seriously will never be very impressed by His grace. They will tend to say, "That sounds okay for the poor guilt-ridden folks who need it. But why should we get all worked up about it? It just doesn't do anything for us." Or, "Yes, yes, we've heard all that before. In fact, we accepted God's grace many years ago. Tell us something that meets our *present* needs." And so the greatest life-changing force in the world is pushed aside as irrelevant. But it is not irrelevant. Take a good hard look at the law of God, and you will see why this is so.

For many of us the term "law of God" brings to mind the general idea of a long list of do's and don'ts. We think immediately of the Ten Commandments: "Thou shalt . . . thou shalt not . . . thou shalt not . . ." Or perhaps we go a step further and think of some of the commands and prohibitions of the New Testament. The Bible is full of them.

But if this is all that the law of God means to us, we have missed the point. A man came to Jesus and asked, "Of all the commandments, which is the most important?" Jesus answered, "'Love the Lord your God with all your heart and with all your soul and with all your mind and with all your strength.' " Then He added that the second commandment is like it: " 'Love your neighbor as yourself.' There is no commandment greater than these" (Mark 12:28, 30–31).

LOVE IS THE HEART OF GOD'S LAW

Here is the point. There *are* do's and don'ts—plenty of them—and we need to obey them. But the whole point of them is this law of love: to love God with all the heart and our neighbors as ourselves. Love is what the law of God is all about. Love is the center around which all other commands revolve. It is the principle that gives them meaning and the reason the other commands were given in the first place. We can never truly understand God's commands unless we see their relationship to the law of love, and we never truly obey them unless we do so out of love. (Compare also Rom. 13:8–10; Gal. 5:14; James 2:8; 1 John 3:11–20; 4:7–21.)

LOVE, A LAW OF THE HEART

This brings us to something else our Lord emphasized about God's law: it must be obeyed from the heart. He says, " 'Love the Lord your God with all your heart' " (Matt. 22:37). He tells us it is not enough to refrain from murder, for "anyone who nurses anger against his brother must be brought to judgement" (Matt. 5:22 NEB). It is not enough to avoid outward adultery; for even the lustful look constitutes adultery (Matt. 5:28). We must make no mistake. Much more is required than mere outward observance of the law. Indeed, heart obedience lay behind Jesus' continual battle with the religious establishment, those who honored God with their lips while their hearts were far from Him. They could adhere rigorously to every jot and tittle of the law, but at the same time oppress the fatherless and the widow and ignore the needs of their own aged parents. They seemed always to find a technicality in the law that got them off the hook.

But what God wants of us is heart love—not just

something external, something superficial, but something
that goes to the very roots of what we are and what we care
about all the way down. In short, love is not love if it is
feigned; it must come from the heart.

THE URGENCY OF THE LAW

To see the law of God in this light is to assent to it and
to know that this law is the world's greatest need. Racial
hatred and the universal social and economic tyrannies shout
to us that more love is needed. Never in human history have
we learned to care enough about others to take the kinds of
steps necessary to ensure continuing mutual understanding,
acceptance, and peace. We don't need to look beyond our
own personal lives—our relationships with our neighbors,
with husbands, wives, parents, children. Who has escaped
the petty jealousies, hostilities, resentments, backbiting,
mistrust, bullying, cringing, false fronts that form so
tragically large a part of almost every human relationship?
None of us truly loves God with all the heart nor our
neighbors as ourselves.

Can God be unconcerned about this state of affairs? He
sees us destroying ourselves and one another by our inability
to love. He sees an almost infinite fund of human potential
being warped, stunted, starved, crushed, destroyed. We may
indeed nourish one another with fragments of the divine
beauty of love, but at the same time we inhibit and quench.
The husband, for all his goodwill, frustrates the potential of
his wife, and the wife that of her husband; and both pass
their neuroses, their immaturities, and their sins on to their
children and their children's children. And so the destructive
chain reaction continues. All the way from Adam it comes
down to the present and threatens to continue unbroken into
the unimaginable future.

If we believe in a personal God at all, we must believe
that He sees and cares. There is no way that He can look
upon us and say it doesn't matter—no way that He can be
indulgent about His law—no way that He can, as it were,
"let us off." He sees the deadly harm we do to ourselves and

to one another, and He knows that only the fulfillment of His perfect law of love will suffice to heal, to give life. To say that He would be content with less than a total living of this law is to say that He cares nothing about the human race and what happens to us. But His purpose for us is unchangeable: He wills our perfection. Nothing less. He will never be content with the travesties of humanity that we now are. He made us to be wholly human, wholly beautiful, wholly like Himself. We are to be perfect, Jesus tells us, "as [our] heavenly Father is perfect" (Matt. 5:48). We are inescapably bound to the necessity, the demand, to love God with all our hearts and our neighbors as ourselves. There is no alternative, no way out. The demands of love are inexorable.

THE PERFORMANCE GAP

Now comes the rub. We see that the heart of God's law is love, and our hearts assent that this must be so, that the law is good, and that our ultimate health and happiness depend on our learning to keep this law in full. But the truth is that we do not in fact keep it. Indeed, we cannot. If we were facing a mere set of do's and don'ts, there might be some among us who could say with the rich young ruler, "All these I have kept . . . What do I still lack?" (Matt. 19:20).

But if it is the full love of our hearts that God seeks, then we are in a sorry state. I don't know of anyone who can look squarely at the requirements of the law of love and feel complacent. We may say how wonderful the Sermon on the Mount is, but I have yet to meet the person who can read the sermon through with equanimity. One doesn't read it and then lean back with a sigh of relief and say, "Is that all? Hurray, I've got it made!" Or, "That's me, Lord! You described me to a T." Instead, we have to take our place with the psalmist, saying, "If thou, Lord, shouldest keep account of sins, who, O Lord, could hold up his head?" (130:3 NEB).

In short, if we take one good hard look at the law of

God and another long look at ourselves, we see a huge performance gap. The law of God is way up there, high in the heaven of God's beauty and joy. But I am way down here in the morass of selfishness and failure. I experience bits of love here and there, to be sure, but even the best of it is tainted and has in it the seeds of destruction. I do not even begin to know what it really means to love God with all my heart or my neighbor as myself.

COPING WITH THE PERFORMANCE GAP

So what can I do? How is a Christian to live with such a performance gap? Well, I can tell you at least three ways *not* to cope with the problem. One is to lower the requirements; another is to grit your teeth and try a little harder; and the third is to throw in the towel and say, "Forget it!" Most of us have tried all three at one time or another. And sometimes we use little bits of all three all jumbled up together at the same time. But mostly we have our deeply ingrained preferences. Each of us has his own characteristic style and emphasis of folly.

LOWERING THE REQUIREMENTS

This is the expedient of sensible people. "After all," they say, "Let's be realistic about this. No one can be perfect. If we're reasonably good guys and try to treat people halfway decently, surely God will understand." But as they say this, their spouses and friends have to take up the slack of their selfishness and irresponsibility, and day by day they write their neuroses and frustrations deep into the hearts and lives of their children. Meantime, racism runs rampant and the brutalities of war and abuses of economic and political power continue. No, God's law cannot be slighted. Our failure to love will always bear tragic consequences, no matter how sensible our attitudes and behavior may seem.

Another way of lowering the requirements is to externalize them. Those who do this do not intend to lower the requirements of God's law. In fact, they may be trying their best to keep the law in all its rigor. But the net result is the same. This is the way of the Pharisees of Jesus' time. They made God's law into an almost interminable list of external do's and don'ts. They tithed mint, anise, and cumin. They fasted. They prayed. They kept the Sabbath. They observed prescribed washings and other rituals. They were not adulterers or extortioners, yet somehow they missed the whole point. They knew nothing of the weightier matters of the law: mercy, righteousness, peace, and joy in the Holy Spirit. The law of love was almost totally beyond their understanding.

Unfortunately, pharisees are still around. And they still have their list of rules—not the same rules, to be sure, but used in much the same way. I remember my list; yours will no doubt be different. Mine included the following: Don't drink. Don't smoke. Don't go to the movies. Don't lie. Don't commit sexual sins. Read your Bible and pray every day. Tell other people about Jesus. Not such bad rules; but often they were little more than that. Just rules. And if people kept them, they could pat themselves on the back and assure themselves that they were pleasing God. They could look around at all the sinners who failed to keep the rules, and know by this that they were among the good guys and the others were the bad guys. "God, I thank you that I am not like other men" (Luke 18:11).

The trouble with such rules is that, with effort, they can be obeyed. You can come to the end of the day and look up at God and feel that you've made it. And you can forget that what God really requires is love and that this command is still a million miles beyond you. You partake of what someone has called the tragedy of the Pharisees: You have a law that can be kept. And the result is that even though you are a total stranger to God's law, you nevertheless convince yourself that you are measuring up to what He expects of you. No, a law so externalized and trivialized can never create in us the beauty that we so desperately need. Such a law can never be God's law.

GRIT YOUR TEETH AND TRY HARDER

Another way that we cope with the impossible demands of the law is to try harder. We have seen that the law of God is good. We know that it must be kept. And we know that mere externals will not do. So we set our sights on perfection as we understand it, and we grit our teeth and drive ourselves to attempt a total and uncompromising obedience. We may not be very honest with ourselves in the process, for none of us can long endure our own inadequacy before the law without a certain amount of self-deception. We may even welcome any indication that others whom we know stand even more condemned before the law than we do; so we may well find something of the pharisee is ourselves.

But, despite our self-deception and pharisaic tendencies, one thing we cannot do: We cannot believe that God is pleased with our present state. So we try our best to do better. Yet somehow every fresh determination to obey the law of God brings its new succession of failures. Every day writes its new catalog of guilt and inadequacy. We confront the duty of prayer at the end of the day, but we can only slink into God's presence. His eye burns and His accusing finger points. We are miserable offenders, and there is no health in us. Nevertheless, day by day, we keep at it. There seems to be no alternative. We labor to keep our bodies under. We whip ourselves. Yet it seems that the harder we try the more miserably we fail. Our Christianity becomes a prison inhabited by a corpse. We are hateful to ourselves, and ahead is nothing but despair. "What a wretched man I am!" we cry with Paul. "Who will rescue me from this body of death?" (Rom. 7:24).

FORGET IT

Still another way of dealing with the performance gap is simply to forget it. We take a look at the pharisee, perhaps, and we say, "Not me! I don't want to be a hypocrite. I'm not going to put on a pious face and pretend I'm better than other people when I know I'm not. I'm not going to be a phony or kid myself that I'm better than I am. And I'm certainly not going to make life miserable for myself like these other poor fools who can't live with themselves unless they do the impossible—who spend all their time knocking themselves over the head because they are such wretched sinners. I don't intend to be either a hypocrite or a breast-beater. There's no way you can coexist happily with the law of God anyway. Forget it! Eat, drink, and be merry, for tomorrow we die."

And so our selfishness continues to flourish unchecked. Our failure to love goes on hurting those nearest to us. And our lack of commitment still allows the fruits of racism and oppression to ripen and breed destruction in all the world around us. No, this is not the answer. It may be better than either of the other alternatives, but it is not good enough. The law of God must be taken more seriously than this.

CLIMBING IN HOPE

Here then is the problem that confronts us: to find some way of coexisting with the law of God, and taking it seriously without either the self-deceit and hypocrisy of lowering its requirements or the misery of self-rejection because of our failure to do the impossible. We need to be honest yet not destroy ourselves through self-hatred. We need to be able to see the law way up there above us and to recognize that we are way down here far below it, but continue to climb in hope, pressing on toward the beauty that lies before us.

But then the question arises: "Is there really any good reason to hope that I ever will arrive? Or even that I will get any closer to keeping the law of love than I am now? And what is God going to do about the fact that I have already broken His law, and still break it? Will He put up with me during the years while I am climbing and have not arrived? And how can I break the habits of years and learn to climb in hope? I seem to have gotten nowhere after all these years. Why should I expect anything different now? Or ever?

WHAT IS GOD LIKE?

The answer to all these questions lies in the answer to an even more important and basic question. What kind of God stands behind the law? What is He really like? And what is His attitude toward me? Is He like a traffic cop waiting behind a corner, watching for every least infraction of the law so that He can zoom out and catch me and cram the rule book down my throat? Is He Big Brother looking over my shoulder? Is He the prime nagger of the universe? Does He give me the cold stare every time I step a hair's breadth out of line? Is He so nasty and perfectionistic about the law that there's no living with Him? Or is He instead the very embodiment of the kind of love He asks of us? Could it be that He is like a truly good father—one who is unalterably committed to seeing us grow up into mature, productive, and beautiful human beings, yet at the same time is a source of support, help, and comfort during the trials of the growing process? Is His concern for us the kind that makes Him impossible to live with? Or is it a joy to have Him near? If He is hard to satisfy, is He nevertheless easy to please?

All these questions boil down to one thing. Is God a hard, legalistic tyrant? Or is He gracious? If He is the former, there is not the faintest hope of any solution to the problem of the performance gap. There is no way that such a God will put up with our struggles during the climbing process and no way that He can teach us to love. But if He is gracious . . .

2 | *UNDERSTANDING GRACE: WHAT IT IS AND WHAT IT DOES*

Here we come to the nub of the matter and to the very heart of the Christian message: grace, the great fact about God that gives substance and meaning to the whole of the Christian faith and life. Here lies the solution to the problem of the performance gap, of learning to live with and obey the law of God. What then is grace?

GRACE: WHAT IT IS

Grace may be defined very simply as unmerited favor. That is, it is kindness shown regardless of whether it is earned or deserved. It is the father welcoming home the prodigal who has squandered his father's wealth on wine, women, and song. It is Jesus welcoming the woman who was a sinner, or saying to the hated tax collector, "Zacchaeus, make haste and come down; for I must stay at your house today" (Luke 19:5 RSV). It is Stephen praying for those who stoned him, "Lord, do not hold this sin against them" (Acts 7:60). It is a patient mother with a sick and cranky child, a solicitous clerk with a difficult customer, an understanding teacher with a dull or obnoxious pupil. It is that quality in the heart of God that causes Him not to "treat us as our sins deserve or repay us according to our iniquities" (Ps. 103:10). In fact it is what love always must be when it meets the unlovely, the weak, the inadequate, the undeserving, the despicable. It responds to need without reference to merit or deserving. It is unmerited favor.

Another way to describe grace would be to compare it with love. Love is, of course, the broader term; for there is a kind of love where grace need not enter the picture at all. You might try to picture a happily married couple in which both husband and wife are all that either one could ever wish the other to be. The husband always respects his wife's feelings, always treasures her individuality, never is unkind, never overbearing. He never treats her like a slave or an inferior, never forgets their anniversary, is a model father, helps with the housework, is genuinely and consistently concerned with her welfare and happiness. She, for her part, returns respect for respect, anticipates his needs, provides a home that is a haven for him, never nags, never undercuts him, always gives freely of her time and concern. The love between the two is always there: genuine, unmistakable, and free, flowing back and forth almost effortlessly in life-giving beauty and power. But grace? There could hardly be any occasion for it. Both husband and wife would be so perfectly lovable that each could scarcely help but love the other.

However, suppose one of the two falls prey to a horrible disease, and becomes subject to ungovernable fits of depression or irritability, unable to care for himself, loathsome in body and unlovely in spirit. Then suppose that the other continues to love just as before, unchangeable in thoughtfulness, undismayed in warm acceptance and concern. That would be grace. And if the love in the first situation had any real depth, it would continue undaunted into the second. Love—if it is genuine love—when the occasion arises, will always be gracious. It cannot be otherwise without denying its very nature. Love, when it meets the undeserving, becomes even more beautiful than it was before. It takes on the new glory of grace.

Still another way to explain the meaning of grace is to say that it is the opposite of legalism. Legalism says, in effect, that you get only what you deserve. It tells you to do certain things or keep certain rules, and then you'll be all right. In any case, love, kindness, favor must be earned.

Grace, on the other hand, gives you what you have not deserved. It pours out love, kindness, favor unconditionally. You don't have to earn it. Earned favor versus unearned. That's the difference.

THE LEGALISTIC HOUSEHOLD

We can see the picture more clearly if we take a minute to look at two imaginary households, one legalistic and the other gracious. Let's say that both sets of parents are deeply committed to rearing their children to be good, moral, responsible adults. They both have family rules for the children. In fact the rules may be very similar in both cases. But somehow in the one family the children have picked up the conviction that they have to earn their parents' love and acceptance. They have to measure up to their parents' expectations. If the children are "good," mother and father will accept them, but if they're not, mother and father will reject them. It isn't hard to see that such a state of affairs is going to have a profound effect on the children. Day by day with each failure or wrongdoing, they find themselves cutting themselves off from something that is scarcely less important than life itself—the love and acceptance of their parents. How are they going to react?

One child will rebel, flouting his parents' expectations, or even setting himself to do everything that his parents want him not to do. He deliberately disobeys. He says in effect, "I don't care what you think of me. My wishes are important to me, and I'm going to do what I want to do." And perhaps down deep inside, he's also saying, "I can't help being bad some of the time. Sometimes I feel downright nasty inside. Please show me that you don't reject me because of that. Please show me that you love me whatever I do."

Another child becomes a hypocrite or a sneak. After all, he cannot afford to show his true face to his parents. If he shows that he feels out of sorts, he gets a sermon. If he does something foolish, he is belittled. If he acts out his anger, he gets put in his place. All his negative feelings and attitudes have to find expression away from home.

Still another child will strive with all his power to please his parents. Yet somehow he never fully succeeds. No matter what he does, he can never quite manage to be perfect or measure up to all their ideals or anticipate their attitudes at every point. So he tries harder and harder, but the harder he tries the less successful he is and the more frequent the failure. At the same time, many of his true feelings may become so unacceptable to him that he learns to bury them deep below the conscious level—to the point where he is no longer even aware of their existence. But he goes on trying to please—not only his parents but others—and slowly grows into a meek, inoffensive puppet who scarcely has any mind or will of his own.

Then there's the foot-dragger. She resents (though she may not understand the cause of her resentment) the unfairness of being forced to do something by an external "oughtness" pressure backed up by the threat of rejection. Her heart simply isn't in the thing that is being demanded of her. And there is no way she can force her heart to be in it. The threat of condemnation or rejection simply doesn't have the power to move her. So she just sits. Eventually she grows into a lump, scarcely moved by joy, sorrow, fear, hope, or ambition—just a passive lump, with almost infinite powers to resist the demands and expectations of those around her.

And there's the incipient pharisee—the child who so fears condemnation that he dare not admit any kind of personal failure, even to himself. Just as perfection of a kind was the price of his parents' acceptance, so it becomes the price of his self-acceptance. As he grows older, failure and its consequent condemnation become so unthinkable that he develops an armor plate against any kind of inadequacy. He has to believe that he is virtually perfect.

These are some of the things that can happen in a basically legalistic home. I have not described all the things that can happen nor have I done justice to the complexities that will be present in any particular situation. Ordinarily, for example, a child will not react simply in one or other of the ways I have suggested, but will combine several of them. Often one type of reaction will be dominant, but there will be others mixed in, too. Furthermore, few homes are wholly legalistic. Usually there will be more wholesome reactions and motivations interspersed with the destructive ones. There are also cases, unfortunately, where there is plenty of grace around the home, but somehow it doesn't get through to the child. He picks up only the elements of legalism and rejection and reacts to them. Each child reacts in a different way, but in each case legalism has been at the root of his problem. The necessity to *earn* the parents' love and acceptance and the accompanying fear of rejection have created a massive central core of insecurity in the child's heart that almost nothing can ease. All his actions, then, are colored by the need to ease this insecurity. The result is that he cannot really become the kind of person his parents want him to be. He can only fake it.

THE GRACIOUS HOUSEHOLD

Look now at a gracious household. Here is a home where love and acceptance are not meted out on the basis of merit. Instead, the parents have somehow conveyed to the child's deepest awareness that their love is not dependent upon his being a good child. Their love is unconditional, unchanging, irrevocable. Somehow he knows that they care about him when he's up, when he's down, when he's good, when he's bad. It is not that they are content with his failures and wrongdoings. They care deeply and they are not willing to settle for irresponsibility and hatefulness on his part. But their unconditional acceptance and love create in the child both the desire and the capacity to please them and to become the kind of person they long to have him be.

I remember a story about a couple in this country who took a war orphan into their home. The child was almost a hopeless neurotic at first. The world had treated him so cruelly that there was an impenetrable wall between him and all the rest of humanity. Behind that wall was a small, lonely, frightened creature, afraid to stick out even the smallest part of his real self for fear he would be crushed, trampled on, and taken advantage of. His behavior, too, was anything but ideal—temper tantrums, disobedience, obnoxious attitudes, and the like. But day after day his foster parents demonstrated that they loved him, that they accepted him despite his unacceptable behavior. Little by little their love began to reach him where he hurt most and his behavior began to change. The temper tantrums slowly diminished, and gradually he began to grow into a different and better person. This is grace and this is how grace works in the heart of a child in a home where love rules.

IS GOD GRACIOUS?

Now that we have seen a little of the meaning of grace as opposed to legalism, we can see a little more clearly why the question posed earlier is so important. Is God a legalist? Or is He gracious? To be sure, the law stands irrevocable. God cannot desire less than our perfection. He knows how deeply we need to learn to love Him with all our hearts and our neighbors as ourselves. But what kind of God stands behind this law? If He is a legalist, if He is going to demand that we earn His favor, if He will reject us at the first failure, we are done for before we begin. There can never be any way of living with such a God that does not breed the destructive reactions I have referred to. To see our failures is to despair. To refuse to see them is either to nourish a pharisaism of the most virulent kind or to practice the most absurd and transparent escapism. God plus moral law minus grace equals death, and our world is full of the dying. The psychiatrists' offices are overflowing with them.

But if God is gracious—if His love and acceptance do not have to be earned, if His favor is free, unconditional, unchangeable, eternal—then there is hope. I do not have to despair when I see my failures. I am not driven into pretending I am somehow better than I am. All of the defense mechanisms that I mentioned as potentially existing in the legalistic home become unnecessary. My security no longer depends upon accomplishing the impossible. I can be what I am without being rejected. I do not have to labor under a cloud of condemnation. I am accepted. I am loved. I can begin to respond to God not merely from the pressure of oughtness but with the freedom of love. I can begin to climb in hope toward the fulfillment of that great law of God.

GOOD NEWS!

Now this is the message that God has given to us in Christ. This is the great good news of Christianity: God is gracious. He is ready to deal with us, not on the legalistic basis of what we have earned, but on the basis of free, unconditional grace. Our God is this kind of God.

This is what Jesus came to tell us: that God loves sinners; that He is like the father who welcomes the prodigal home. No recriminations for unfilial behavior or for his debaucheries. No I-told-you-sos. No cold politeness. Instead, the joyful embrace! The fatted calf! The feast! "For this son of mine was dead and is alive again; he was lost and is found" (Luke 15:24).

Not only did Jesus *tell* us what the Father is like. He showed us in the graciousness of His own behavior. He freely consorted with the tax collectors and the sinners, not in self-righteous superiority, but in a love that won their hearts (Matt. 9:10–13). He ate in the home of Zacchaeus, the hated tax collector (Luke 19:1–10). He conversed with the despised Samaritan woman (John 4:7–30). He accepted the "woman who had lived a sinful life," and allowed her to wash His feet with her tears, even amid the heavy condemnation of onlookers (Luke 7:36–50). He silenced the accusers of the woman taken in adultery, receiving her with those incomparable words, "Neither do I condemn you . . . go now and leave your life of sin" (John 8:11). Finally, He gave His life, "the righteous for the unrighteous, to bring [us] to God" (1 Peter 3:18). And, dying, He could look even upon those who were crucifying Him and say, "Father, forgive them, for they do not know what they are doing" (Luke 23:34). In grace He had come "to seek and to save what was lost" (Luke 19:10), "and to give his life as a ransom for many" (Mark 10:45). He had not come to call the righteous, but sinners (Matt. 9:13). Both in deed and word, both in life and death, Jesus demonstrated the meaning of grace—so much so that John, who perhaps knew Him best, could say of Him, "We saw his glory . . . full of grace" (John 1:14 NEB).

But the important thing is this: that by all these things that Jesus said and did, He was showing us something about *God*. The glory of grace that John saw was the glory, "such glory as befits the Father's only Son." No one had ever seen the Father before, but "God's only Son, he who is nearest to the Father's heart, he has made him known." He was "full of grace," and from Him believers "have all received grace upon grace" (John 1:14, 16 NEB). This then, is the wonder of the Christian message: that God is this kind of God; that He loves me with a love that is not turned off by my sins, my failures, my inadequacies, my insignificance. I am not a stranger in a terrifying universe. I am not an anomalous disease crawling on the face of an insignificant speck in the vast emptiness of space. I am not a nameless insect waiting to be crushed by an impersonal boot. I am not a miserable offender cowering under the glare of an angry deity. I am a man beloved by God Himself. I have touched the very heart of the universe and have found His name to be love. And that love has reached me, not because I have merited God's favor, not because I have anything to boast about, but because of what He is and because of what Jesus has done for me in the Father's name. Further, I can believe this about God (and therefore about myself) because Jesus came from the Father and has revealed by His teaching, by His life, by His death, by His very person that this is what God is like: He is "full of grace."

GRACE TRANSFORMS

Now this fact about God is more than just a heartwarming truth. It is more than mere insurance against an unpleasant hereafter. It is a fact that transforms a person. It changes his motivation and makes him new. And this happens, not because God reaches into us by magic, as it were, and overwhelms us by an act of sheer unexplained power, but because it is the very nature of grace to do this. Grace, simply because it is grace, changes a person.

This happens even on the everyday level of human relationships. Remember, for example, how grace changed the war orphan—how it untied the knots of fear and frustration in his heart and began to make him a different boy. Similarly, my wife's gracious love for me frees me to become a better, fuller, stronger person. Even a dog will become a better creature if its master, in some sense meaningful to him, loves him and does not reject him because of his misbehavior or doggy limitations. That's what grace by its very nature does.

Once more, Jesus shows us how it works. In grace He accepts Zacchaeus, and what is the result? Zacchaeus' heart is changed, and spontaneously he says, " 'Here and now, sir, I give half my possessions to charity; and if I have cheated anyone, I am ready to repay him four times over' " (Luke 19:8 NEB). Jesus accepts the "woman who was a sinner" in the house of Simon, and forgives her sins. And what happens? A new love is born in her heart—the result of a natural law that says a person who is forgiven much will also love much (Luke 7:47–50). That's what grace does to a person.

The apostle Paul repeatedly emphasizes the same thing. In one place he tells us, in effect, that grace destroys the power of sin: "Sin shall not be your master," he says, "because you are not under law, but under grace" (Rom. 6:14). In other words, deliverance from the power of sin is the necessary result of being out from under the law principle, and under grace instead. Later, Paul goes on to tell us what being under the law or legalistic principle does: It kills. "The very commandment that was intended to bring life actually brought death," he says (Rom. 7:10). He has tried to keep the law and found that he cannot. In his impotence, he has been driven step by step to that bitter cry of anguish, "What a wretched man I am! Who will rescue me from this body of death?" (v. 24). Who indeed? But then comes the answer: "Thanks be to God—through Jesus Christ our Lord!" (v. 25). And so Paul passes into a new world where he can cry out with joy and certainty, "Therefore, there is now no condemnation for those who are in Christ Jesus" (8:1). He has passed from the implacable, death-dealing demands of the law to the "no condemnation" of grace; and in passing, he has discovered that what the law could not do because of his own sinful nature, God has done through Christ. God has found a way of fulfilling in him the requirements of the law (8:2–4). Grace has made the difference!

Elsewhere, Paul tells us, "the written code kills, but the Spirit gives life" (2 Cor. 3:6 RSV). I here equate "written code" with the legalistic principle, and "Spirit" with grace. This is warranted from the context, for throughout the chapter Paul compares the old dispensation of law, and its resulting condemnation, with the new dispensation of life in Christ. And the significant thing about the new regime under the Spirit is the fact that it is not legalistic and condemning. It does not lead to judgment and death for every infraction of the law. That is, it is founded upon grace. Under it even the worst sinners find life. (Concerning the equating of the term *Spirit* with the term *grace*, see also Gal. 3:1–5.) Then he goes on to say that under the new dispensation (grace) a veil has been removed between God and us (2 Cor. 3:16), and now we can see Him clearly. As we do so, we are "being transformed into his likeness" (2 Cor. 3:18). That is, we become more like God. In short, to be exposed to the new dispensation of the grace of God is to become more godlike. God's grace changes us. This is what grace does and always will do when it touches the heart.

IF WE BELIEVE

There is, however, one absolutely inescapable condition that must be met if grace is to change a person. Grace must be *believed*. It has to be met by an answering trust. To explain, let me go back to my story about the war orphan. The grace of the orphan's foster parents enabled him to change and to break out of the prison of his insecurity and fear. But this could happen only when the child came to the point of opening his heart in trust. Without trust on his part, all the grace and acceptance in the world would have done him no good at all.

Try to imagine how the child might have reacted to his foster parents' kindness if he could not trust their goodwill. Perhaps he would say to himself, "I wonder what these people have up their sleeves. I know all about their kind. Smooth as butter on the outside. They get you to stick your neck out, and then they lop your head off." Or perhaps he would say, "None of this mushy love stuff for me. They just want to stick their noses into my private business. Then when I tell them all about myself, they'll start telling me what to think and when to breathe. No, thank you!" Or again, "I don't know why these people think they have to be so nice to me, but I'm going to make the most of it. I'm going to ride the gravy train for all it's worth."

All these the orphan boy might have said to himself before he came to see the love of his foster parents for what it really was. But as long as he could not open his heart to their love—as long as he saw in their kindness nothing but self-interest or treachery or the need to dominate or gullibility—there was no way that love and kindness could bring a change for the better. It is simply an inescapable fact of life that love expressing itself in gracious behavior will not bring heart renewal and change to the one who receives it unless that love is perceived for what it really is and unless that love awakens heart trust. It is not the love that's lacking; it is simply that love is powerless unless it is welcomed with trust. A thirsty person may have at hand enough water to swim in, but if he is afraid to drink, if he cannot believe the water is safe, he must remain thirsty.

This is why the Scriptures make so much of faith. "Believe, and be saved." "Whosoever believes . . . " "To everyone that believes . . . " Over and over again we are confronted with the same demand. It's not that faith is something so magical or mystical. Nor is there anything arbitrary about it—as if God were more pleased with people who can spout the right dogma than He is with changed lives, or as if faith were the pound of flesh that God extracts from us before He is willing to bless us. No, God is totally committed to writing His law on our hearts; and the love that will produce this change is there, unconditional, inexhaustible, ready to give life to any and all—ready to give itself unstintingly for the very worst of sinners. But even the love of God Himself is powerless to enrich our lives if we cannot trust Him. In fact, if God cannot be trusted, His love must, of all loves, be the most unwelcome. If I cannot trust Him, if I do not really see Him as gracious, then He becomes Enemy Number One. The very fact that He is God and all-powerful makes Him of all persons the most to be feared and perhaps even hated. Furthermore, if God is not worthy of trust, then there is no conceivable way that I can accept His love and His grace and be refreshed or changed thereby. His very kindness is deadly. He is the ultimate foe. Who can tell what fearful purposes and ulterior motives lie behind His pretense of goodness?

But if I can know that God is totally trustworthy, that His love is absolutely real, that His kindness is utterly sincere, that His concern for me really does mean abundant life, then His grace can do that which is its very nature to do. It can reach me where I really live. It can transform me. It can touch the very deepest motivating drives of my heart and make me a new person.

And this is the very thing that God is committed to do for us. He intends to write the new covenant upon our hearts. He wants to do, by grace, what the law could never do—to fulfill in us the demands of the law. He wants to enable us to learn what it means really to love Him and to love our neighbor. He wants to make us like Himself. And it is by grace that He does it. The Father, because He is gracious, loves us while we are yet sinners. The Son, by His life, His teachings, and His death personally demonstrates— out where we can see it—what that gracious love means. And the Holy Spirit takes that truth revealed by Christ and applies it to our very hearts so that we can understand it, believe it, and be transformed by it.

FROM THE LORD WHO IS THE SPIRIT

This work of the Holy Spirit lies at the very heart of the Spirit's ministry. Paul tells us, for example, when he talks about our being changed "with ever-increasing glory," that this comes "from the Lord, who is the Spirit" (2 Cor. 3:18). The Holy Spirit is the one who does it. This is *His* work. Then in another place Paul describes the qualities of this new life as "the fruit of the Spirit" (Gal. 5:22). In other words, new life isn't born of the clenched jaw and the iron will. It doesn't come through agonizing or through great efforts of commitment and self-abnegation. No, the Holy Spirit opens our eyes to the wonder of God's gracious love, and when grace touches the heart, the new life simply grows, natural, free, and sweet. It is the *fruit* of the Spirit. (Note too that Paul tells us about the fruit of the Spirit only after he has spent almost the whole of the earlier part of the letter to the Galatians explaining God's grace.)

In still another place, Paul writes that the law finds its fulfillment in us as we walk "according to the Spirit" (Rom. 8:4) and that He gives life "through his Spirit, who lives in [us]" (Rom. 8:11). Again, we read that God gives strength and power "through his Spirit in [our] inner being" as we "grasp how wide and long and high and deep is the love of Christ" (Eph. 3:16–18). This is what the Holy Spirit lives within us to do. He's not here to condemn or to nag. He's not here to overwhelm us or to swallow up our individuality nor to make spectacular outward demonstrations of divine power—though He may on occasion do so—nor to administer infusions of divine ecstasy. He's here to reveal to us, to make real to us, the glory of the grace of God in the face of Jesus Christ so that we may see, believe, and be remade, transformed, changed into Christ's likeness from one degree of glory to another. This comes from the Lord who is the Spirit.

TRANSFORMATION IS A PROCESS

I have stressed the fact that grace, when answered by faith, produces transformation and that this transformation comes through the grace-revealing work of the Spirit. But it needs to be understood, further, that this change is not complete all at once. It is a process. As Paul says, we are *being* changed into God's likeness "from one degree of glory to another." Or, as Peter says, we are to "grow in grace" (2 Peter 3:18). In other words, this business of transformation takes time. It is never fully consummated so long as we live here on earth. To be sure, there is a time when we pass from darkness into light, from despair into hope, from imprisonment to freedom. But the whole of the promised land is not won in a day. There are still giants to fight and cities to take. Very much land remains to be possessed. To put it another way, we do not become completely like Christ the moment we believe or even the moment we surrender wholly to Him. We have not yet fully learned to love as we are loved. We have not yet attained, but we press toward the mark. We are not sitting around rejoicing in our perfection; we are still climbing in hope. I repeat: The grace-faith transformation that I speak of is not an instantaneous event but a continuing process.

THE BEGINNING OF THE PROCESS

The process must, however, have a beginning—a time when we pass from spiritual death to spiritual life, from alienation apart from God to a living relationship with Him. Before that relationship begins, God's love is meaningless to us. We ignore Him or we hide from Him or we walk in terror before Him, burdened with a weight of condemnation that no assurance, no effort can remove. He is, at best, a stranger; at worst, an enemy—the ultimate enemy. There is no way we can love Him, and His very presence makes it impossible to love either ourselves or anyone else. Then the meaning of His grace dawns upon us. We find that He is not what we had thought. We had looked for judgment, but we found love—a love that could give all, that could surrender its very lifeblood that we might live. And, having seen that gracious love, having understood it and believed it, all is made new. As the song writer says,

Heaven above is softer blue;
Earth around is sweeter green.
Something lives in every hue
Christless eyes have never seen!

We have passed from condemnation to acceptance, from fear to favor, from law to grace, from death to life. Love has reached out and touched us, and by its very sweetness love has awakened an answering love in our hearts. We have, in Jesus' words, been born again. We have become a new creation. Old things have passed away and all things have become new.

But the important thing is the fact that it is grace that initiates and causes this change, this new birth. Peter tells us that we are "born again, not of perishable seed, but of imperishable, through the living and abiding word of God." Then he adds, "That word is the good news which was preached to you" (1 Peter 1:23, 25 RSV). And what is the good news but the message of God's grace? Paul writes, "If anyone is in Christ, he is a new creation" (2 Cor. 5:17). Then he goes on to say that from first to last this has been the work of God "who reconciled us to himself through Christ . . . not counting men's sins against them" (vv. 18–19). Again grace—a perfect description of it. Then in another letter Paul tells us that we were once dead in sins but now we have been made alive by grace (Eph. 2:1–9). It's grace that does it every time. You can write it down that when one sees God's grace for the first time, and believes it, a new life has begun.

It is well to remember, however, that this new birth, this beginning of the transformation process, is not manifested in the same way for everyone. For one person, the change may be spectacular and all but instantaneous. Just like Paul. One day he is persecuting the church and breathing out threatenings and slaughter against those who believe. The

next day he is praying and calling Jesus *Lord*. Within a week
he is powerfully convincing the Jews that Jesus is the Christ.
For another person, the emergence of the new life may be
totally different. It may involve a long, underground
germinating process, moving almost imperceptibly into the
quiet sprouting of a new faith and a new way of life. One
may be able to point to the very day and hour when the new
life began. But another cannot. He only knows that, whereas
once he was blind, now he sees. He may not even clearly
remember a time when he did not love the Savior. Yet he
does love Him, and he knows that he has tasted of the grace
of God and that for him the new life is here. It must have
begun sometime, but he cannot tell when. Regardless,
however, of how the new life is begun, we have Jesus' word
that begin it must. We *must* be born from above. And this is
what God wants to do for us; He is in the business of
creating new people, of giving new life, of transforming us
through grace. And that recreating, that transformation,
begins when we first see the grace of God revealed in Christ,
as it is made known to us through the Spirit, and when we
first open our hearts to Him in trust.

THE PROCESS CONTINUED

But, as I say, the transformation is far from complete. It
takes time to develop and mature. We have indeed been born
again. We have done an about-face, and life will never be the
same again. But now come the years of slow, patient
growth. As Peter says, we must ". . . grow in the grace and
knowledge of our Lord and Savior Jesus Christ" (2 Peter
3:18). Or, to use Paul's words, having begun in the Spirit
(that is, as he makes clear, on the principle of grace through
faith), we are to finish on the same basis (Gal. 3:1–3). Again,
as he says in the passage already quoted several times, "We
all . . . beholding the glory of the Lord, are being changed
into his likeness from one degree of glory to another; for this
comes from the Lord who is the Spirit" (2 Cor. 3:18 RSV).
You see, the transformation does not happen all at once. It
keeps on and on and on. We have not yet arrived. We are not

perfectly in His likeness. Nor will we be until we see Christ face to face. We are not "already perfect," but we "press on" (Phil. 3:12). There is not one of us to whom Peter does not need to say, "Grow in grace." There is no point in this life at which we no longer have any further degrees of glory to realize in the transformation process.

Why is this so? Simply because we have not yet discovered all that God is and all that His grace can mean for the changing of our hearts and lives. We do not yet see Him as He really is. We do not yet know the full splendor of His graciousness. And so the unconquered territory in our lives yet remains. Now we see "only puzzling reflections in a mirror" (1 Cor. 13:12 NEB), and so our lives reflect His glory only dimly. We made one discovery of His grace yesterday, and this changed us a little. Today we see Him a little more clearly, and His grace changes us a little more. Tomorrow there will be still new perceptions and transformations. We are all being changed from one degree of glory to another as we behold Him. But, to repeat, we do not yet see Him as He is, and because we do not yet see Him as He is, we are not yet fully like Him.

THE PROCESS COMPLETED

But some day we *will* be fully like Him. Some day we will see Him with no obscuring veil between, no mists of ignorance, no cloud of misunderstanding, no fog of unbelief. When that day comes, we know that we shall be like Him, for, as John tells us, "What we will be has not yet been made known. But we know that when he appears, we shall be like him, for we shall see him as he is" (1 John 3:2). That's what will do it. No great abracadabra act of power. Merely (how can we think of it as "merely"?) the blazing splendor of the full sight of what He is. That will be enough to make all the old rags of our imperfections, sins, and inadequacies drop off like a discarded cloak. But now? Ah, yes, the long, seemingly endless upward climb of a lifetime of learning to know and appropriate His grace. Here a little, there a little. Now crawling. Now slipping. Now making heartwarming leaps. But always making new discoveries about Him so that as we behold Him, we will be changed ever more into His likeness from one degree of glory to another. This is the life to which the Holy Spirit calls us, and for which He strengthens us as He shows us the things of Christ, for this "comes from the Lord, who is the Spirit." And some day? Yes, we will become fully like Him, for we shall see Him as He is!

3 | LEGALISTIC HEART HABITS

At this point you may well be saying to yourself, "This is all very fine and high-sounding. But why doesn't it work? How is it that we can look at the church, or (what's more to the point) at ourselves, and see so little of this transforming power?" We would do well to ask this question of ourselves. Not once or twice, but over and over again. It is a question that cries out for answers.

Let me share with you some of the obstacles, pitfalls, and roadblocks that I have discovered, one way or another. I can speak with some authority at this point because there is scarcely an obstacle that I have not run afoul of! There is scarcely a mistake that I have not made—and made it gloriously, life-size, full color, and in three dimensions.

Undoubtedly the biggest roadblock—one, in fact, that includes all the others—is the fact that our minds and hearts, from earliest childhood, have developed certain habitual reactions toward God, toward righteousness and good behavior, and toward our own inadequacies and failures. These reactions dominate our attitudes and feelings throughout the various demands and vicissitudes of life. Furthermore, these habits of reacting and thinking are often profoundly legalistic. That is, despite all that our minds—and even our hearts—may tell us about the grace of God, these blind, unreasoning habits lead us to react as if somehow we had to earn something from God, as if God is, at some level, condemning us for our sins and withholding His love and acceptance until we do better.

I remember a vivid illustration in my own life of the strength of my heart habits. Soon after my breakdown, I began to see in a new way that grace lay at the heart of all of God's dealings with us. I began to see that the gospel, the very thing I had been preaching all my life, was the one thing I had failed to appropriate at the everyday motivational level. I realized clearly that in my thinking and attitudes I had misrepresented God and His purposes in my life, and that I would have to discover, or rediscover, a different kind of God. But when it came to actually doing this, I found it well-nigh impossible. I wanted to have a relationship with this different kind of God, this God as He really is, and not as I had earlier felt Him to be. But I could not. Every time I opened the door to some kind of fellowship with Him, the old heart habits reasserted themselves. Even with my new-found understanding of Him, there was no living with Him.

The net result was this: I simply had to leave God alone for a while. Of course, I was emotionally very ill at the time. But it simply was a fact that anytime I tried to let God into my life, I fell apart at the seams. I had to go it alone, and this aloneness went on for many months. I finally reached the point where all faith in God was gone. I did not even know whether God existed, and I didn't see how I could ever know. So I found myself alone in a spiritual desert. It was in some respects a better place than where I had been living shortly before, but it was anything but pleasant. All my life I had felt, in some sense, an awareness of God's love and presence. Even in the darkest hours of my breakdown, I had believed that somehow, sometime, God would bring me back to a life of hope and meaning. But now this consciousness was gone. I was alone in a faceless universe. I yearned for a long drink of living water. But I found none.

The day finally came when I was able to let God back into my life again. I was riding in a bus at the time when all of a sudden it came to me that God was near, that I could talk to Him, and that He would hear. I also suddenly knew, with new force, that I didn't have to swallow all the things

I'd always been taught about Him, and that He would receive me even with my doubts and misunderstandings. So for the first time in many months, I prayed. What a release! A sense of joy, assurance, and fellowship with God flooded through me such as I had never experienced before. The prodigal was home again.

But home did not stay homelike. The first day after that experience was great. The second day was fairly good. But after that things kept getting worse and worse and worse until finally I was down at the bottom all over again. Here, for months, I had gradually been getting away from the emotionally destructive aspects of my breakdown. Little by little I had started to be human again: to be able to work, go to school, enjoy recreation, make decisions. Yet scarcely a week from the day I let God back into my life I was beginning to disintegrate again. The only solution seemed to be to forget about God and go it alone once more. So I did. And again I experienced the spiritual drought. Again the return to God. And again the slow spiral downward. Over and over again this cycle repeated itself. Why?

At the time, I did not understand very well what was going on. But with the wisdom of hindsight I can see in large part what the trouble was. I was up against the old problem of obedience: "If you love me, you will obey what I command" (John 14:15). So I tried to keep what I thought (often mistakenly, I'm sure) were God's commandments, only to meet with repeated failure. And upon the heels of failure came self-hatred and despair. The worst of it was that I could not very well sort out God's attitude toward me from my own. This is where my religion was so deadly. I had a God who was the epitome of warmth, forgiveness, and understanding when I had been reduced to despair, hopelessness, and raw need. But once I undertook to live for Him, there was no pleasing Him. I simply could not do well enough in my Christian life to maintain fellowship with Him. In other words, fellowship was not something that sprang from mutual love and acceptance; it was something earned. I had to perform up to a certain level before I could win the continuing sense of His love and acceptance. So even though I knew in my mind that God was gracious, yet at the heart-habit level I acted as if He were not. I was a legalist through and through.

Perhaps few have ever had such a virulent case of legalistic heart habits as I had, but I suspect that nearly all of us are afflicted with such habits to some degree. Way down in the dark of our subconscious or semiconscious feelings the old habits and attitudes hide and fester. Continually they steal back and reassert themselves, destroying as they come. Whenever things don't go well or whenever the old wound of our inadequacies is touched to the quick, back come the old reactions: the old anger, the old rebellion, the gossip, the criticalness, the peevishness, the lust, the arrogance, the lumpish passivity, the self-justification, the slavish resentful obedience, the depression, the despair, the self-hatred. But at the bottom of it all is the old legalism. Somewhere we have lost sight, again, of the grace of God. God has become someone who will not accept us unless we are perfect. It's not fallen men and women like us He loves, we say in effect, but only perfected beings far above what we can ever hope to be.

Furthermore, I suspect that each of us has his own particular type of legalistic God—a God who reacts a certain way when we fail to earn His approval. Perhaps your God is like the traffic cop mentioned earlier. He pays little attention to you when you are obedient to the law. But if you do something wrong, out He comes and chases you until He gets you. Or perhaps He's a recordkeeper, as in the old song: "He hears all you say, He sees all you do; my Lord's awritin' all the time." No misdeed escapes Him.

Or perhaps your God is a nagger. All day long it's, "Why did you do this?" Or, "Why didn't you do that?" Or, "Why aren't you a better Christian?"

Perhaps your God is what I call "Old Stonyface." You know the type. You're going along having a good time, talking, laughing, and so on. Then somehow you touch a sensitive area and the person you are with freezes up on you. Then silence—cold, condemning silence. Only apologies and abject self-abasement can get you back into his good graces again.

Possibly your God is like a domineering parent. He wants to control every breath you draw. Every decision is to be his alone. Every thought, every feeling must be forcibly made to conform. All individuality is to be crushed; for how can you, so foolish and sinful, lift up your head in the presence of omniscience and perfect righteousness? So God becomes not the gracious father leading His children to maturity, but a tyrant who dominates, controls, crushes, smothers. No one can live with such a God and continue to trust Him or long believe in His grace.

GRACE AS A WEAPON

One of the most horrible distortions of God's true nature is that which makes God into the kind of person who uses His love and grace as a weapon to force obedience. In other words, grace becomes not so much a fact of His very nature, the way He naturally behaves and in so doing wins my love and obedience. Rather, grace is something God does *for* me, and then throws it in my face to put me under obligation to do all sorts of things I have neither the inclination nor the resources to do. It's as if God were to say to me, "Look what I did for you. Now why aren't you a better Christian? Have you no gratitude? You ought to be ashamed of yourself! Get with it!" And out comes the whip.

The dreadful thing about this kind of God is the fact that when He treats us this way, He seems to be altogether right. We indeed ought to respond to His kindness with greater love and commitment. Our ingratitude *is* despicable. We haven't a leg to stand on. Yet somehow grace has disappeared from His dealings with us, and because grace is missing, our very reason for responding properly to Him has withered away. Grace has tried to compel a response by ceasing to be grace and it just doesn't work.

Imagine someone saving your life by a great act of self-sacrifice and heroism, and then later using this act of heroism against you. To begin with, you are so grateful to your rescuer that you would do anything for him. So when he comes to you a couple of days later and asks to borrow some money, you gladly agree. Then a week later he comes back and says, "I hate to ask you this, but I've been needing a car for some time now, and I've found just the one I want. Do you suppose you could help with the down payment? It comes to about a thousand dollars." This time you gulp, but you say, "I'm not sure I can get ahold of that much money, but I'll certainly do what I can."

A couple of days later he returns and says, "My wife needs to get away for a week or so. Could you baby-sit for us?" You hesitate a minute but then reply, "Well, it will be a little difficult; we had hoped to be out of town." He turns on you with a reminder. "Ahem. Is there any chance that you could change your plans? It's embarrassing to have to say this, but you know I did save your life." "Oh, dear," you say with a sigh. "If you put it that way . . . I'll see what we can do."

And so it goes on, week after week. One time it's additional financial help. Another time it's helping with work on his house. Another time it's running errands for his wife. And with each new demand your reluctance grows, and as your reluctance grows he increases the pressure. More and more frequently he reminds you of what he did for you until finally you can't stand it anymore.

"What if you did save my life?" you say. "What's the good of living under this kind of burden? Why can't you just leave me alone? It would have been better if you had just let me die that day!" And you slam the door in his face. You've been used long enough. The great fund of goodwill you once had has dried up because the other person's kindness has been used as a weapon against you. Farfetched? Perhaps. But some of us have a God not greatly different from this— a God who once died for us but who now never ceases to use that act of kindness as a weapon to force our obedience.

And some of us have a God who uses our own love against us. You perhaps have seen a parent do this to a child. One moment the child is cuddling up to his mother, throwing his arms around her, telling her how much he loves her. Then she firmly disentangles herself from him, glares at him, and says, "Well, why aren't you a good boy then?" And something in the child's heart dies.

Is it any wonder that many Christians, after repeated pleas and cajolings to respond to God's grace and to demonstrate their love to Him, find their gratitude quenched and their love motivation all dried up? This kind of grace— if it can be called grace—has no life in it. It only destroys.

BEGINNING AND END-POINT GRACE

Another problem or roadblock that is closely related to what I have just been talking about is the problem I call *beginning and end-point grace.* This is an attitude or approach toward Christianity that puts grace at the beginning of the Christian life and grace at the end, but, in effect, puts almost nothing but legalism between.

In this approach there is no question about grace at the beginning. There is plenty of it. No sinner is too low for that grace to reach, and there's great joy over any sinner who repents. When testimony time comes, each Christian goes back to that wonderful time when God first saved him. He will never forget that joyful day in such and such a year, on such and such a month, day, and hour when God's grace touched him and everything was made new. No lack of grace there.

There's also plenty of grace for the ultimate future. When the books are opened, my name will be there. I don't need to fear hell anymore. Grace has delivered me from the final judgment. I know that in that hour there will be no condemnation for me. Jesus paid it all.

But what of the years between? All too often it is nothing but deadly, grinding legalism. God is, in effect, telling us, "Look what I did for you back at Calvary. Look how I accepted you and forgave your sins when you first believed. Look what I've promised you as your reward in heaven. Now let's see you act accordingly. Let's have a little more gratitude. Get busy!" Or perhaps we sense His saying, "Look here. I'm in the business of saving sinners, but I'm not going to tolerate the least bit of sin among My children. If you want to have fellowship with Me, you'd better watch yourself. You don't need to think I want you around unless you get thoroughly squared away and keep yourself that way." And so God, the insatiated Taskmaster, drives us on to keep doing the good works that we have neither the desire nor the power to perform. Like some of Paul's converts, having begun in the Spirit, we now seek to be made perfect by the flesh (Gal. 3:3). Grace has become a mere conversion mechanism, a fire insurance policy. It may be good news for the fearful saint upon his deathbed. But it's not good news for us every day. It's not something that makes life wonderful and God a joy to live with. It's grace for the sinner, but law for the saint. Justification grace but sanctification legalism. God's grace has lost its everyday transforming power.

PERFECTIONISM

Another problem—and one that lies at the root of many others—is that of perfectionism. By that term I do not mean the drive toward excellence that almost all of us have. There need be no harm in a desire to work a math problem correctly. A pianist, if he is going to amount to anything on the keyboard, must continually strive to play every note correctly and to put in all the proper dynamics. Nor is there any harm in a person's wanting to learn to be a better husband and father or a better wife and mother. In fact we need very much to strive toward that perfect love for God and for one another that we all lack. As Jesus said, we need to be perfect as our heavenly Father is perfect (Matt. 5:48). Indeed, life on earth could be seen as simply a matter of pressing toward a perfection that we can never fully attain.

When I talk about perfectionism, it is not this reaching out, this pressing forward to a higher goal, that I am referring to. Such striving is essential to growth. What I refer to is that attitude that makes perfection the prerequisite for acceptance, that says, "I cannot accept myself if I in any way fall short of perfection." Along with this attitude is the

crippling conviction that other people will not accept me
when I fall short. And behind it all is the dreadful feeling that
God will not accept me either. He may be willing to save me
from hell, but only at the cost of wiping out nearly
everything that is really me. Meanwhile, until that wiping-
out job is completed, He finds me little better than a nasty,
dirty object. I am so far from perfection that almost
everything I am and do displeases Him.

The person who is a perfectionist in this sense is by
definition a legalist. He has to earn self-acceptance and God's
acceptance and others' acceptance by being perfect. He has
stepped out of grace ground altogether. It is not sinners
whom God loves (or if He does, it is a love distorted to
meaninglessness); God loves only perfected saints. He is no
longer gracious. He is a legalist, pure and simple.

LEARNING GRACE HEART HABITS

The above are just a few of the non-grace heart habits to
which many of us are prone. There are more, but perhaps
these are enough to help us see and understand some of the
attitudes and ways of thinking that all too often bring
destruction into our lives and render the grace of God
ineffective. What can we do about these heart habits?

First, we need to improve our concept of God. We need
to see the areas in which our perception of Him is so
tragically inadequate. Then we must raise our sights to
something beyond, something higher, something incompa-
rably more beautiful than anything we have yet dreamed.
We need to cry to God with Moses, "Show me your glory"
(Ex. 33:18). And having seen some small portion of that
glory, we must realize with Moses that it is only His back
that we have seen (v. 23). We have not yet seen the beauty
of His face. We have not yet been fully transformed by that
beauty so we press on toward the time when we shall see
Him as He is, and then become fully like Him.

Second, we must continually reaffirm our trust in God's
grace. We must consciously take our stand over and over
again on grace ground. When we feel the condemnation of

others, when we fail, when we feel inadequate, when we are frustrated and out of sorts, when we feel like dirt in our own eyes, at all times, again and again, we need to remember that "this also God loves." God does not share our low opinion of ourselves. He does not add His voice to other people's condemnation. We are not dirt to Him. We are His children, loved, cherished, accepted. We are His. And He is gracious.

4 | ROADBLOCKS: LEGALISM IN THE HOME AND IN THE CHURCH

Up to this point I have been dealing with roadblocks to grace that are set up because of our own heart habits and attitudes. There are others that come from outside ourselves—our parents, teachers, friends and acquaintances, the society we live in, and from the church. Most of us already are very good at setting up these roadblocks for ourselves; we don't need help from outside. But, like it or not, we have such help anyway. Plenty of it!

THE LEGALISTIC HOME

Unfortunately one of the most powerful sources of non-grace ideas and attitudes is the home. It is here, often, that legalism gets written into our very bones. The trouble is that children have minds and ways of their own. At times they can be almost unbelievably loving, kind, and endearing. But at other times they seem to have an enormous capacity for destructiveness, selfishness, and folly. Part of the parent's job is to try to help the child choose the one and shun the other.

At best this is an extremely difficult task to do effectively. If the parent doesn't take the child's selfish behavior seriously enough, he is more or less asking for the child to grow up selfish. But if the parent spends most of his time battering away at the child's selfishness, or if he deals with it in the wrong way—especially the legalistic way—the child may just get his back up or he may learn a kind of external "goodness" that in no way springs from the heart.

We have already seen some of the effects of the legalistic home upon the life and attitudes of a child. Let us now look at some of the ways in which this legalism or non-grace is conveyed. Remember that legalism is that attitude or way of dealing with a person that says in effect, "You must *earn* my kindness, acceptance, or love. I will accept you only if you behave properly or perform adequately. If you fail or fall short, you are to be condemned and rejected." Scarcely any parent will subscribe fully to this way of treating a child. Nevertheless, something of this attitude gets across, and this something infects the child's entire life, perhaps permanently. How then are these attitudes conveyed?

THE WORM TECHNIQUE

One way is by the use of the worm technique. The parent wants the child to shun evil and do good; so when the child does something bad, almost the only thing the parent knows to do is to make the child feel like a worm, like a nasty something. So he pours on the guilt: "You *naughty* girl!" Then comes the paralyzing glare, the sermon, the tongue-lashing; and the child writhes about like a bug on a pin or shrivels up like paper scorching in the fire. Happy is the child who can become inured to such treatment.

Not that the child necessarily is free from guilt or from the need for repentance. He may need very much to understand where he is wrong and to turn to something better. But under the worm technique, any change of behavior will be for the wrong reasons: to escape anger and condemnation, not because the child is learning to trust and obey his parents or to love truth or to be considerate of others.

BLAME-PINNING

Another way to convey legalistic attitudes is the habit of blame-pinning: "It's all your fault." Someone has to be made to see that he is the source of the trouble. Since the fault is so often shared, a game readily develops where the blame is tossed back and forth: "I didn't do it, she did." "Well, he hit me first." But the blame has to be pinned on somebody, and when the game is over, any genuine sorrow that anyone might have had for hurtful behavior is dried up.

OUGHTNESS PRESSURE

Another way is what one might call oughtness pressure: "You *ought* to have . . . " "You *ought* not to . . . " Now, there are indeed things that one ought and ought not to do. I ought to pay my just debts. I ought not to help myself to someone else's property. Little Jimmy ought not to punch his sister in the eye. Seven-year-old Sally ought to ask her mother's permission before going to spend the day at Janie's house. The point is not whether such oughts exist or whether they should be taught, but how one deals with them and whether at the same time one is instilling in the child the values behind the oughts.

The danger comes when life for the child becomes little more than a matter of duty: Do your duty and you are acceptable. Fail and you are not. Then later when the child comes to learn about God, this God becomes little more than the enforcer of oughtness, the omnipresent Taskmaster behind the law. With such a God, there will never be enough love and grace to awaken the faintest genuine desire to do what *ought* to be done.

NAGGING

Another conveyor of non-grace is nagging. When you want to get a child to stop doing something bad or to start doing something desirable, you nag him. All day long it's "Why did you do this?" "Why didn't you do that?"

The child also learns that no matter what he does, he will never be good enough to escape the demands, the criticisms, the sermons. Likely as not, he builds up a defense of stubbornness and insensibility against all of it. Then when

God comes along with His catalog of expectations, His claims also become dull, negative, carping irritations that have not the slightest power to motivate the child or to remake him into something new. Grace has been nullified by the heart's automatic reaction to a nagging God.

REJECTION PUNISHMENT

Yet another conveyor of non-grace is the use of various kinds of rejection as a tool to modify unacceptable behavior. You give the offending child the silent treatment, you set him in a corner, you send him up to his room as unfit for human society.

One needs, of course, to be very sensitive to a child's reaction to punishment. A child may interpret punishment as rejection even when no rejection is meant, and what conveys rejection to one child may convey little or none to another.

THE PARENTAL PERFECTION MASK

Some parents teach their children legalism by habitually wearing a mask of perfection. That is, the parent never acknowledges his own fallibility, weakness, or failings. In his dealings with the child, he always acts as if he were perfect—almost godlike in his wisdom and behavior. The child readily sees through this pretense. He sees the lack of consideration, the unkindness, the rudeness, the arrogance. He may not understand why his parent behaves like this, but he does know that he is not being treated as he should be.

In the long run, such behavior may destroy the child's confidence in his parents. But it has other unfortunate effects that are just as harmful. The child may, for example, learn to despise himself. Whenever there is disagreement, friction, or misunderstanding it is always the child who is made to feel in the wrong. Often the result is that he develops a miserable self-image. He learns to think of himself as no good, as inadequate, as the kind of person who is never fully able to earn the love and acceptance of others. Then when he meets a God who really *is* perfect, he misunderstands that perfection and finds himself unable to win God's acceptance also.

Another unfortunate effect of the parental perfection mask is this: The child learns by his parent's example to wear a mask of his own. He learns that the best way to deal with his own failures and inadequacies is simply not to acknowledge them. He never learns what it means to be a fallible human being living among other fallible human beings, all learning to accept themselves and one another as they really are. He never learns that it is safe to acknowledge his faults. He never learns the constant renewal of openness or the joy and release of confession and forgiveness. No one has ever shown him how.

APPEAL TO DIVINE AUTHORITY

One of the most deadly ways of teaching legalism is that of bringing God in to support the parent's authority—using God as a threat to compel obedience: "God will punish you for that." "Remember, He sees everything you do, even when Mother isn't around. So you'd better watch your p's and q's." Now the child does need to learn that God sees everything, and that He is opposed to sin, but there could hardly be anything more destructive than imparting this knowledge as a threat or as a rider to a rebuke for wrongdoing. With God pictured as a hostile power that one cannot escape, there is no way that the child will ever come to see the beauty of His holiness or be renewed by an understanding of His grace. God is for him the great threatener, the ultimate legalist. Nothing could be more foreign to His nature than grace.

OTHER LEGALISTIC INFLUENCES

Having seen above some of the ways in which non-grace is imparted to the child in the home, it is not hard to see that the same kind of influences abound elsewhere. The child goes to school and learns legalism from his teachers. And before long he discovers that society in general is run on a legalistic basis: Be good and you're okay; be bad and you're rejected. Then when the child grows up and gets married he finds that his spouse treats him the same way. To be sure, at first, in the flush of new love, he finds an acceptance that he never dreamed possible. But with the passage of time and the slow discovery of mutual and seemingly ineradicable faults, both husband and wife gradually return to the legalistic standard. More and more they demand certain improvements in each other as the price of acceptance, and they begin to reject one another in various ways because of unacceptable behavior and character traits. So love begins to wither. The habits of a lifetime have taken control again.

THE LEGALISTIC CHURCH

Given the prevalence of legalism in so many aspects of life, it should not surprise us that sometimes the church itself becomes an agent of non-grace—perhaps even a very powerful one. And the legalism is often intensified by the church's concern with the problem of human wickedness and sin. Indeed, the church *should* be concerned, for all of us need—and desperately need—to learn to live by God's law: to love God and one another. The church that did not concern itself with such matters could hardly call itself a church. The trouble is that the church may be composed of people who, in almost all of their relationships, have learned to be legalists: Be good and you're okay; be bad and you're condemned. And when a legalist gets hold of a problem of morality, how can he deal with it except legalistically? The more important morality becomes, the more pervasive and deadly the legalism grows.

To put it another way, if you are not overly concerned with morality or sin, you don't have much to be legalistic about. If morality doesn't matter a great deal, why go to all the bother of rejecting yourself or anyone else because of failure? Of course, if other people's failures happen to hurt you or threaten you at some point, you may feel called upon either to retaliate or to give the offenders a wide berth. But there's no need to be shocked at the dreadful, immoral behavior that goes on all around you—no need to draw a line between your small group of righteous friends and the wicked, wicked world outside.

But if morality does matter, if sin is a vital issue, then the legalist turns to condemnation and rejection as naturally as breathing. The more important morality is, the more severe the condemnation and the more unyielding the rejection. In fact, I am convinced that law (or morality) plus legalism equals death. There is no way around that fact. There is no alternative. And the church, unfortunately, all too often demonstrates the truth of the fact. Instead of being a fountain of life it becomes a power for death. The moral law of God, distorted as it is, occupies such a large position on stage that grace finds almost no room at all.

This is a dreadful thing to say about a church—any church—and it may be that few churches are as profoundly legalistic as I have been describing. One certainly hopes so. Yet I fear that few fellowships of believers have fully escaped all taint. And being tainted, it is only natural that, one way or another, church members will convey their legalism or non-grace to each other.

EMPHASIS ON EXTERNALS

One way of conveying non-grace is by overemphasis on external behavior. When I was a young man, many of the church circles I frequented had a list of external things that a "spiritual" Christian simply did not do: He didn't smoke, drink, dance, play cards, or go to movies. It's true that sometimes, perhaps even often, these things were indeed given up as a step of genuine commitment to God. But that's not the point. The trouble was that these abstinences were considered to be the mark of the spiritual or committed Christian.

The tragedy is that so many of the weightier aspects of the law became of lesser importance. The outward, obvious things received the most attention, and these were the things that instantly gauged a person's spirituality. You didn't have to know the secrets of a person's heart before you knew him to be immature, shallow, uncommitted.

JUDGING IN THE CHURCH

Even when we manage to avoid overemphasis on externals, there is still plenty of the judgmental, non-grace spirit around. Unfortunately, we don't require the sanction of a set of explicit rules and prohibitions before we can find occasion to condemn and reject one another. This is what lies at the heart of legalism; if any of us fails to measure up, he's to be condemned and rejected. And in many ways we effectively condemn or judge one another and do our bit to destroy the powerful working of God's grace in another's life.

GOSSIP

Perhaps the most common way of expressing judgment upon our brothers and sisters is gossip. Someone does something improper or unchristian, and, oh, how quickly the word spreads! "Have you heard what the pastor did to Ned Wilson?" "I hear the Robinsons aren't getting along very well with each other. Isn't it a shame?" "I think Mrs. Clarke is stepping out on her husband. I wonder what he'd do if he knew it." And so the stories spread, getting more and more sinister as they are passed on. What perverse pleasure we take in reporting these stories—half-commiserating and half-savoring the weaknesses and sins of others, boosting our own self-image at the expense of someone else's, and judging them in the process.

Sometimes even prayer meetings become an occasion to gossip. Regretfully, we speak to one another of the sins and failings of those not present. Earnestly we pray that God will deal with the matter. But beneath the pious sorrow and concern is the self-righteous pleasure of our own spiritual superiority and the need to expose the weaknesses of a brother or sister in Christ.

EXCLUSION

Another way we condemn or reject others is by shunning, ignoring, excluding people who don't measure up or who disagree with us or who aren't our kind. Perhaps someone does something we don't like, and we say in effect, "If he's going to be that way about it, let him! See if I care! He can go his way and I'll go mine." And so we exclude a brother in Christ from our fellowship and our love, putting him down as not worth our time. We judge our brother and at the same time teach him the meaning of non-grace.

THE PUT-DOWN

Some of us, instead of gossiping or shutting out our fellow Christians, specialize in the verbal put-down. Directly or indirectly we suggest that such and such behavior is inexcusable or that anyone with any sense or commitment to Christ would do so and so. Or perhaps we argue a point in such a way as to put down our opponent. Sometimes we couch our opinions in broad, preferably scriptural generalizations; but all the time we have in mind someone who is behaving contrary to what we feel "ought" to be done. Behind all our pious words is the spirit of condemnation.

CONDEMNING THE UNCOMMITTED

Some of us, especially officers of the church, express our condemnation indirectly by continual pressures on others to be more committed or more involved in the program and activities of the church. One way or another, we are continually asking, "Why aren't you in the choir?" "Why aren't you more faithful in church attendance?" "You ought to give more money to the church."

It may very well be true that more commitment is needed. But so often behind our behavior, behind our questioning, lies a spirit of condemnation and oughtness that kills in others the very thing that could make them want to join heart and soul with the program and ministry of the church.

Pastors are perhaps more susceptible to this disease than anyone else, for their own ministry is judged by the success of their efforts to get people involved. But nobody wants to get involved except the faithful few. Still, the pastor keeps on trying, but the harder he tries the more lifeless everything seems to be. Finally, the pastor's nagging degenerates into scolding. Sunday after Sunday he upbraids the people because they are not better Christians. Other pastors may avoid the snare of scolding but deliver one sermon after another on commitment. "Give your life more fully to Christ." "Rededicate yourself." "Get involved." Chiding, pressure, demands for more commitment—all these in plenty; but little or nothing of the glory of the grace of God that moves the heart and wins men and women to the commitment that is so urgently necessary.

PERFECTIONIST DEMANDS UPON THE PASTOR

But let us not blame pastors too severely. While they, in word or in spirit, are condemning people for their lack of commitment, we are shoveling the condemnation back onto the pastors with at least equal vigor. Perhaps no one in our society lives in such a goldfish bowl as does the pastor. He must be a nearly perfect Christian, and everyone has an opinion of what a perfect Christian is. Everyone else can be excused here and there, but not the pastor. In his private life he is to be the perfect husband and father, yet no one allows him the time that being a perfect husband and father demands. In his professional life he must exercise a greater variety of gifts than God ever gives to one person. He has to be effective at visitation, counseling, administration, community leadership, and the like. Then after we've forced him to spend forty to fifty hours a week on these things, we still expect good, thought-provoking sermons from him every Sunday morning. Happy is the pastor who is so solidly grounded in the grace of God that he can walk unscathed through the furnace of ever-present criticism without becoming embittered or degenerating into a people-pleaser or leaving the ministry for freer, more rewarding work.

THE SPIRITUAL MASK

Another symptom of non-grace is the wearing of a spiritual mask. You quickly learn that there's a lot of condemnation around for the person who doesn't measure up to what a good Christian and church member should be. So you make sure that you project the right image. You wear a mask. For example, for many years I wore the mask of a nice guy, devoted to the Lord's work, in love with His Word, walking in sweet fellowship with Christ, with each thought and each motive under the Holy Spirit's control. Not that anything was wrong with these as ideals, but as pieces of my mask they were deadly.

The fact is, when you imagine (as a part of your act) that you are measuring up to the current set of expectations in your church group, you so easily get to thinking of yourself as a part of the spiritual elite. You even pray earnestly for those who do not yet "have the victory." And conversely when you feel you aren't measuring up, fellowship with God's people becomes a most painful experience. You try to smile the same sweet, spiritual smile, and pray the same deep, earnest prayers. But the effort chokes you. You feel that every eye can pierce the façade and see the shallowness beneath. But it never occurs to you to open up—except perhaps as a very painful kind of confession that you hope will earn you the smile of God and the approval of your brothers and sisters in Christ.

Often one finds so little grace in the church, so little unconditional acceptance! Everyone simply has to keep his pious mask fixed as tightly as possible. In fact, all too often, the church is the last place where it's safe to be totally honest, to be exactly what you are, to be exposed, unmasked, and unadorned. We sing stirring songs about the grace of God who accepts us just as we are. But we don't accept one another that way. And the church, the very body that He created to transmit the grace of Christ to His children and to the world, becomes a powerful force that undercuts the very meaning of that grace.

DEALING WITH ROADBLOCKS

How can we face the magnitude of the task that confronts us in learning to allow the grace of God to become a truly life-changing force? How are we going to cope with these roadblocks? How do we respond to all the non-grace around us? How do we deal with the power and the fruits of legalism in our own lives?

Let me say first that one response to these roadblocks will not help in the least. That is to start pointing the finger: "My parents are nothing but legalists." "My husband doesn't have the faintest conception of the meaning of grace." "The church is legalistic from top to bottom." "The pastor preaches nothing but legalistic sermons." "There's no use wasting your time with that crowd; they're such thoroughgoing legalists that the only thing you can do is pull out and leave them to play their little church games."

Do you see the danger? You fight legalism, condemnation, and rejection by answering in kind. You draw your holier-than-thou robes about you and complain about the lack of grace in others. It seems that our hearts are so non-grace oriented that even when we hear about grace it becomes merely a weapon to condemn our brothers and sisters who have not yet been enlightened.

The answer is to teach grace by demonstrating it. You don't cure the legalist by condemning him. You cure him only by showing him in word and deed the unconditional acceptance of grace. This does not mean that there need never be occasion for rebuke. In fact, rebuke works only when it is delivered humbly in the spirit of grace.

There's another type of response to roadblocks, especially those that arise in your own heart, that simply won't do. That is to start pointing the finger at yourself. Perhaps you've heeded my oft-repeated contention that grace produces change in the heart and life. But you look at yourself

and don't see much change there. So all my talk about grace
has only intensified the guilt. You conclude that you
obviously don't have the combination. Perhaps you aren't
even a Christian after all. So you respond by giving up hope.
What's the use anyway? You'll never get anywhere. Or
perhaps you haven't quite reached the stage of despair so you
start trying to do better. You try to prove by your actions
that you really *are* a child of God; you really *have* received
God's grace; you really *do* love Him. But the unease down in
your heart keeps nagging at you. You can't quite quench the
fear that you may be only kidding yourself.

If this is the way you feel, I can only say that grace is
what you need. You need to see it, believe it, and rest in it.
Until you do, there will be no significant heart change in
your life. It may be that you have never really encountered
the grace of God at all, never really met the God who
receives sinners just as they are. Or it may be that you really
have met Him, but His grace somehow has been smothered,
buried under the various pressures and demands of life. I can
only tell you to come to the fountain of grace and find rest
and renewal there. Don't try to prove anything. Don't try to
pump up the works that will show how much you love
Him. Face it. The chances are that as long as you are unable
to rest in His grace you don't really love Him at all. For you
there's nothing about Him that could win your love. But
open your heart to His grace, and you'll find you love Him
without trying. And your life will begin to show it.

One more suggestion: If you find it hard to trust and
live trusting God's grace, my guess is that you need at least
one Christian friend to whom you can open up about your
problem—one who will show you what the grace of God
means, simply by accepting you as you are. Most of us find
it difficult to believe that God really accepts us as we are
when for all of our lives we have not found that acceptance
from people we've known. Even the apostle Paul, when he
was first converted, needed someone like Ananias to come
along and say, "*Brother* Saul."

If you are having grace trouble, don't try to tough it out
on your own. Even the best of us cannot manage it.

5 | *STILL ANOTHER ROADBLOCK*

Before I leave the subject of roadblocks to grace, I must deal briefly with a roadblock of a different kind. This last one is something that sometimes passes for grace, but it is not the real thing. It's spurious. It's a so-called grace that tells you it doesn't matter how you behave. You can sin all you like and everything will be all right, for God accepts you as you are and He will forgive you.

Let me affirm just as emphatically as I can that this is *not* what I am teaching, and it's not what the Bible teaches. Grace is not the same as license. It will never teach us to "go on sinning so that grace may increase" (Rom. 6:1). Rather, it takes sin and God's law with utter seriousness, and then it enables us to begin to keep that law. Anything that claims to be grace yet fails to lead in this direction is spurious grace. It falls miserably short of God's gracious purposes for us.

GRACE TAKES SIN AND GOD'S LAW SERIOUSLY

The truth is that grace, as taught in Scripture, never takes a cavalier attitude toward sin. In fact, grace is what it is only because God's law, and our failure to obey it, are matters of utmost urgency. It's because our sin is so heinous and so deadly that grace comes to us as such a glorious, liberating, life-changing gift of God.

To show you what I mean, let's suppose that you have

done something truly dreadful to me, and then you come to me and say you are sorry. I forgive you and accept you into a deep and continuing relationship with myself. That would be a forgiveness and acceptance that means something. It would be a genuine grace that would make a difference in your life. Suppose, on the other hand, that your offense had been something trivial—something that I didn't really care about one way or another—and then I made a great to-do about forgiving you. What could my forgiveness possibly mean to you? It would be empty. It would be cheap. It would turn you off. For if sin is trivial and unimportant, then so is grace. But if sin is a matter of utmost seriousness and importance then so, too, is grace. The measure of sin is the measure of grace. As Paul says, "Where sin increased, grace increased all the more" (Rom. 5:20). That's what makes God's grace so incredibly wonderful.

Now let me carry the matter a little further. Suppose I had forgiven you for this terrible wrong, and then you used my forgiveness as an occasion to go right on doing the kind of things you had done before. Suppose you said to yourself, "Well, it doesn't make any difference how I behave. I can do anything I like. I'll be forgiven in the end so what does it matter?" Such behavior could mean only that my forgiveness, my acceptance meant nothing to you. It hadn't reached your heart. You hadn't really been touched by it. It was nonsense to you.

So grace is not something that frees us to go on sinning to our heart's content. We come to God's grace in the first place only because we have seen the urgency of His law and the awfulness of our sins, because we have been shaken to the core by the knowledge of what we ought to be and are not, and because we long for release from the sins that are destroying us.

GRACE FULFILLS THE LAW

This brings me to my second point: grace is not a way of doing away with the law but of fulfilling it. Paul tells us, for example, that the grace way does for us what all the demands and prohibitions of the law could never accomplish. It delivers us from the prison of our sins "in order that the righteous requirements of the law might be fully met in us, who do not live according to the sinful nature but according to the Spirit" (Rom. 8:4). Only grace can do this. Guilt, condemnation, judgment, the relentless hard line— these can never produce the righteousness that God requires. As I've said before, they can provide a kind of outward morality. But true heart righteousness? Never! Law, by itself, cannot produce the fruits that law demands. It can only kill. But grace, by its very nature, produces both the desire and the power to do what the law requires. It writes God's laws upon our very hearts. Grace does it, and grace alone. If something comes along that calls itself grace yet fails to do this or at least begin to do it, that is not genuine grace. It's a counterfeit. It's a lie. Grace can and must produce heart change, once it is answered by true heart faith.

6 | DEALING WITH THE PROBLEM OF SIN

So far, I have been trying to describe the grace of God from a variety of angles—the need for it, what it is, how it works, how it is expressed, how it is blocked, and the like. But I have not touched on what is, perhaps, the most important aspect of all: that the basis of grace is found in the atoning death of Christ. Stressed over and over again in Scripture is the fact that God's grace to us is possible only because of the shedding of the blood of Christ. For example, in Romans 3:24–26 we read that we "are justified by God's free grace alone, through his act of liberation in the person of Christ Jesus. For God designed him to be the means of expiating sin by his sacrificial death, effective through faith. God meant by this to demonstrate his justice, because in his forbearance he had overlooked the sins of the past—to demonstrate his justice now in the present, showing that he is himself just and also justifies any man who puts his faith in Jesus" (NEB).

Again, in John 1:29, we find Christ called "the Lamb of God, who takes away the sin of the world!" This obviously refers back to the Old Testament system of sacrifice where a lamb had to be offered and killed on the altar to atone for sin. Again, in Ephesians 1:7–8 we are told that in Christ we have "redemption through his blood, the forgiveness of sins, in accordance with the riches of God's grace that he lavished on us." Clearly, for some reason Christ had to die before we could be forgiven. All forgiveness prior to that time looked forward to that atoning sacrifice, and all forgiveness since then springs from it.

WHY THE CROSS?

This raises a problem. If, as I keep insisting, grace changes people, does that not in itself solve the sin problem? Surely Christ's very graciousness, when I come to know it, washes the sin out of my life and writes God's law upon my heart. Why then does my sin require expiation or atonement? Why does someone have to die for it? If God is so kind that He wants to forgive my sin and accept me as I am into His family, why doesn't He just do it? Why does He have to look around for an innocent victim to punish before He'll let me off the hook? Is He so legalistic that when someone slaps Him in the face He has to slap back or else find someone else He can vent His fury on? Is He not content with merely eradicating sin in me by His grace? Must He still find someone to punish?

THE NEED TO DEAL WITH SIN

It would all be incomprehensible but for one thing—the nature of sin and its consequences. It's sin that does it. This thing in us is so monstrous, so insidious, so deadly, that only the death of God's Son could stand against it and give deliverance. Why so?

Well, for one thing, if it is not dealt with, sin by its very nature blocks the operation of grace. I said earlier that grace cannot produce heart change unless it is believed. It is equally true that grace cannot do its work unless the sin that obstructs it is seen for what it is and repented of. Suppose, for example, one has been forgiven for deliberately and maliciously ruining the reputation of his friend, yet he refuses to face up to what he has done. This very refusal, this callousness, blocks any healing or life-giving effect the friend's gracious forgiveness might have had. His friend's grace has come to him at great personal cost, but that grace is meaningless to him. He has never faced the enormity of what he has done. The sin problem has never been dealt with.

And what could we say about a grace that did not stop the harm that sin does to the innocent? Imagine a con man who has robbed a dozen widows of their life savings being brought before a judge who tells him, "That's all right, brother. We're all sinners here. I'm prepared to accept you as you are if you'll do the same for me. How's that? Does it make you feel and act a little kinder toward others? So run along now, and try to do a little better next time. You really must be more considerate of other people."

Obviously, again, such behavior will not do. It ignores the miseries of the widows who have been wronged or who may yet be wronged, and it does nothing for the man himself. To put it bluntly, this kind of grace is nonsense, for sin has not been taken seriously and fully dealt with. Let us therefore look at the sin problem a little more closely.

THE NATURE OF SIN

A simple definition of sin might be that it is any disobedience to the two great commandments: first, that we are to love God with all our hearts, and, second, that we are to love our neighbors as ourselves. Now we are so used to living in a world where no one really keeps these commandments—where everyone, when the pressure is applied, gives himself the edge over his neighbor—that we can never really see the enormity of this disobedience. We never see where it ultimately leads.

At worst, this disobedience, this sin, amounts to living in what we might call a one-self universe. Other selves, of course, exist. But only one self is intrinsically important. *I* am important. The others are important, not in themselves, but for my sake. Their importance consists only in their potential as conveniences for my comfort, tools for carrying out my purposes, food to satisfy my hunger; or otherwise as rivals to defeat or enemies to placate, avoid, or if possible stab in the back. In the final analysis, all other selves are either actual or potential enemies, and God, of all persons in the universe, has to be Enemy Number One. How could it be otherwise? Here is One who cannot be defeated, cannot be avoided, cannot be used. And above all He cannot be trusted, for He is bigger than I am and He has desires and purposes that are bound to run counter to my own. If the two of us exist in the same universe, I have no option but to rebel, hide, or yield a false, servile obedience. Yet in the long run all expedients are bound to be equally futile. What is there to do but hate such a One?

This, then, is what it means to live in a one-self universe. Surely it is this very spirit in human nature that led Paul to say long ago that "the outlook of the lower nature is enmity with God; it is not subject to the law of God; indeed it cannot be; those who live on such a level cannot possibly please God" (Rom. 8:7–8 NEB).

THE UNIVERSALITY AND SERIOUSNESS OF SIN

Obviously, what I have been describing is sin at its worst, and we might be tempted to think that none of us is like that. After all, look at how much genuine kindness there is around. Look at the acts of heroism and self-sacrifice. Look at all the warm productive relationships we have. Look how responsible we are as parents, spouses, workers, citizens. We're not such a bad lot. Oh, we do have our faults, and sometimes we can get pretty nasty. But by and large we do reasonably well.

And it's true that there is a good bit of genuine love to be found. None of us lives wholly in the one-self universe I've been talking about. But the trouble is that we've all got some of it in us. The very fact that we, being what we are, can still defend ourselves and turn the accusing finger aside, is proof that the evil within us has not been seen for what it is. It has not been dealt with. For there is something of that one-self universe in every single one of us, and its destroying power dulls the beauty of all our relationships, sets a ceiling on our aspirations, and, collectively, casts its pall on our national and international affairs.

Two facts lead me to believe the one-self universe attitude is much more deeply entrenched in our hearts, much more deadly than any of us is willing to recognize. One is what happens to us when we band together in large masses: governments, large business enterprises, labor unions, and the like. I have never heard, for example, of any large group of people who, without external pressure or necessity, willingly agreed together to suffer major inconvenience or loss for the benefit of other groups who were worse off than themselves. (I do not consider American aid to foreign countries as a case in point. Our giving has never hurt us nearly so deeply as the recipients of our bounty are hurting because of their needs, and who can say that external pressure or self-interest might lie behind the giving?) When the chips are down, expediency almost always wins out over morality. Nations and large groups of people have always, with a clear conscience, been able to do the most outrageous things to other groups—things that few of us would ever do to another human being in private life. I've often heard it said, for instance, that many of the perpetrators of atrocities in Nazi Germany were good husbands and fathers.

That's one of the tragedies of the human condition. People in the mass look out for their own interest in the most shameless fashion. The only thing that ever stops them is power. Even the United States Constitution recognized this. Power must be checked by an answering power. There have to be checks and balances to set limits on the selfishness and rapacity of large, powerful groups of people.

The second fact that reveals our selfishness is what happens to people in a group when they are faced with circumstances of the kind found in some of the prison camps and internment camps during World War II. I think, in particular, of events in a camp in Weihsien, Shantung, China, where I myself was interned for a couple of weeks before being repatriated. The story is told by Langdon B. Gilkey in his book *Shantung Compound*. This was a camp in which all internal affairs were managed by the prisoners themselves: assignment of living quarters, work details, distribution of supplies, law enforcement, general administration. The only problem was that there was not enough food, fuel, or living space to meet the felt needs of the people. The result was that each one looked out for himself, each family for itself; and almost without exception, people treated others unjustly in the process. Yet they were often unable even to see the injustice and selfishness of their own behavior. There was always a good, moral reason for what they did.

The point of all this is not that those men and women were so much worse than others. Rather, it is the fact that any of us, when pushed to the wall, can become like that. There is a wild beast within us that, given the chance, will come out and show its true disposition. We have to face it: Our sin is not a mere inconvenience or a mild misfortune. It is a deadly disease that needs to be cured. It is something within each of us that must be rooted out, eradicated, killed.

THE CONSEQUENCES OF SIN

The trouble is, of course, that sin has consequences, both to ourselves, to the particular people we hurt, and to the society in which we live. It hurts us because every misdeed shapes us. Every harm we perpetrate upon another person leaves its corresponding twist or flaw within us. By doing the harm we not only express the kind of persons we already are, we also write the defect more deeply into our own nature. Something that God created to be beautiful thus becomes more and more warped and corrupted.

Of course sin also hurts others besides the wrongdoer. That's the dreadful thing about it. If I kill another in anger, I not only destroy the person himself, but I cause tragedy and pain to his widow and his fatherless children. Even my tamer sins do their deadly work. What I am pleased to call my little foibles—my neuroses—leave a permanent mark on my wife's character and on my children. From me my children acquire the distortions in their personalities and pass them on in turn to their children. Thus the iniquities of the fathers are indeed visited upon the children "to the third and fourth generation" (Ex. 20:5). Sin does not confine its hurt to the sinner himself. It goes on and on and on hurting people.

And the hurt spreads to the whole of society. What seem to be little selfishnesses here and there are not dissipated when they spread out into the wider circle. They are compounded. They lead to oppression, enslavement, economic and military imperialism, war, famine, poverty, misery, death, torture. And it's not just the system that's the problem, evil though it may be. It's the sinful people that make up the system, people just like you and me. There's never been a system that ever brought in true happiness and love because no system ever has or ever can adequately deal with the problem of sin and its consequences.

This is why God has to deal so drastically with sin. If He cares about the world He created, He must either purify the sinner or judge him: purify him by taking away his sinful heart or judge him by terminating his time of probation and ensuring that his sin will no longer hurt anyone but himself.

HOW IS GOD TO DEAL WITH SIN?

But if God is going to purify the sinner, He will have no shortcuts. To make me pure by an act of naked, divine power would be little better than divine rape. Such disrespect for His own creation has never been God's way. The only alternative is to bring us to the point where we can see with our own eyes and our own hearts the meaning of sin, and to turn from it. Somehow we have to be made to see the enormity of sin, and all its deadly consequences. We have to see that sin matters, and that God will never in time or eternity let the matter of sin slide. For if He lets it slide, where is His righteousness? And if He allows sin's dreadful consequences to go unchecked, where is His love? Yet if He punishes the sinner, what then? Punishment, in and of itself, seldom produces genuine repentance. And in any case, no punishment short of ultimate loss is serious enough to deal with the reality of what sin is. Where would that leave us? To all these questions there was only one answer. Calvary.

THE CROSS EXPOSES SIN FOR WHAT IT IS

Only in Jesus' death at Calvary do we see the sin problem for what it truly is. We see, for example, its murderous consequences—the fearful extreme to which it drives the sinner. We see what happened when the Son of God came to His people in His humility and in His passion for righteousness. Most people didn't even recognize Him! The religious establishment became enraged when He sought to show them a new and better way; and they finally arrested Him, tried Him on trumped-up charges, and put Him to death. Not just ordinary death, but crucifixion—the ultimate in pain and degradation. Rome, the military and political power of the day, washed her hands of the injustice; yet she supplied soldiers to do the deed—to mock, torture, and finally kill the Son of God. Even the common people who once heard Him gladly joined the throng to scream for His death.

But we miss the point if we draw back in outrage at those people who joined to crucify the Savior. We all have that in us which, if given its head, would do the same thing. If Jesus were to come to the United States today, would we all hear Him gladly? Would we like some of the things He would have to tell us? I have not the slightest doubt that, if He were to speak to us today in person, many of us would find our deepest selves threatened. Sooner or later we, too, would howl for His blood. We, too, are unwilling to have this man rule over us. We, too, want to keep our share of the proceeds of the vineyard we are pleased to call our own. And we, too, are unwilling to give God His due, even when His own Son comes to collect. As long as any one of us prefers himself before God or others, as long as we insist on giving ourselves preferential treatment, this is where we will find ourselves when the chips are down and when we are driven to the wall. In the end our self-centeredness will lead to the destruction of anything and everyone that stands in our way—even to the killing of God's very Son. This is what our sin means.

We need to see this clearly. We need to see beneath the

mask of our own self-righteousness, beneath the veneer of respectability, beneath the veil of what we imagine we are when everything is going well in our lives and nothing is threatening us. We must see our preferential treatment of ourselves for what it is—a seed of the tree of hell, which, when it is grown, will seek to overtop and smother all other trees.

Calvary helps us see this. It helps us see the deadliness of sin. It helps us see where self-love leads if it is ever given its full scope and if it's not repented of and rooted out.

SEEING WHAT SIN DESERVES

To see what sin leads to is also to see what sin deserves. For surely, if sin is going to cause someone suffering, it ought to be the sinner himself who suffers. He is the one who deserves it, not the innocent victim.

If I hit you in the eye, I ought to be the one whose eye hurts. It's not right that *you* should have a black eye when *I* am the one who did the wrong. In fact, that's why you are so ready to hit me back. And that, surely, is why the Old Testament had a law that demanded "eye for eye, tooth for tooth" (Ex. 21:24). But I'm afraid that your retaliation doesn't really solve the problem. If you hit me back, I may wind up with a black eye just like yours, but it doesn't really help *your* black eye at all. You still have one, and it still hurts. And after you've given me my black eye, I'm not a bit more likely to feel sorry for what I've done. I'm just as likely to want to give you another one. Yet the point remains: *I* ought to be the one to suffer for my sins.

Yet when I look at Calvary, it is not I who suffer. Someone else is enduring the consequences of *my* wickedness. The Son of God Himself hangs on the cross because of other people's wrongdoing. The Pharisees and Sadducees or the Roman soldiers should be hanging there. *Humankind* should be crucified. It's *our* kind of behavior that brought Him there. It's we who should be suffering the pain. It's we who should be crying out in agony, "My God, my God, why have you forsaken me?" (Mark 15:34). Why should He, the sinless One, suffer this, the Just for the unjust?

The only possible answer is that God chose it. God would have it so. God knew that letting sin go unpunished wasn't the answer. How would we ever see the deadliness of it and repent? He knew that hitting back wasn't the answer. It would only magnify the hostility and alienation. And God knew that punishing us was not the answer, for punishment in and of itself so seldom leads to genuine repentance, especially when meted out by someone whom you don't know and trust. Besides, what kind of punishment would answer? Only the ultimate punishment could ever match the seriousness of the offense or stop the deadly consequences of our selfishness. But where would that leave us? Where then would be the possibility of repentance and redemption?

GOD TURNS THE OTHER CHEEK

So Calvary was all that remained. Sin had to be seen for what it was. And at Calvary we see it, unmasked, unrestrained, doing its worst. Sin had to have its day, and it did, in all the horror of its deadliness. God, as it were, had to turn the other cheek. When Jesus was the One wronged, there was no "eye for eye, tooth for tooth." Only love and forgiveness for His enemies. Sin, indeed, had to be judged. Someone had to take responsibility for its consequences. And Someone did.

JESUS ASSUMES OUR GUILT

But this was not merely a matter of someone's taking a beating that someone else deserved. Humanity was on trial. We were the sinners. We were the kind of people who would do this to God's Son. But Jesus, as man, took the responsibility for what we are and what we have done. He, as man, assumed the guilt of the rest of us. He, as head of the race, stood with us, just as the head of any organization or family takes the rap for wrongs done by those under his charge. When Jesus dies there, He doesn't say, "Father, look what they've done." Rather, He says, "Look what *we* have done." So "for our sake God made him one with the sinfulness of men, so that in him we might be made one with the goodness of God himself" (2 Cor. 5:21NEB). He "died for sins once for all, the righteous for the unrighteous, to bring [us] to God" (1 Peter 3:18). Was ever love like this?

GOD WELCOMES THE SINNER

The wonder of it all is that Calvary, the ultimate expression of human sin, the last straw of our alienation from God, turns out to be the very thing that brings us back to Him. By it we see the deadly seriousness of sin. God is not sloughing it off as if it didn't matter. But He Himself endures its worst consequences so that we can see sin for what it is and at the same time have a relationship with Him. We see our desperate need for repentance, and at the same time we see hope for ourselves. Love will welcome us— sinful though we are—and will keep on cleansing us, keep on working with us, until we are fully free from evil, until we truly have His laws written upon our hearts, until we become wholly like Him in love. This is grace.

7 | *FREEING THE REAL ME*

In the last chapter I dealt with the problem of sin, for when all is said and done, the sin problem is precisely what grace is all about. However, people react to this problem in various ways. Some seem unable to take it very seriously. Even while giving lip service to the Christian teaching about sin and its deadly consequences, they still feel that at heart they are pretty nice people. Oh, they have their faults, but doesn't everybody?

THE WORM VIEW OF HUMAN SELFHOOD

On the other hand, some Christians take the problem of sin so seriously that they go to the opposite extreme. They adopt what I call the *worm stance*: "I'm such a dreadful sinner. There's absolutely nothing good in me. Everything has been totally corrupted by sin. I'm just no good at all."

To such people, this position seems easily justified both by experience and by Scripture. In their day-by-day living they've found that no matter how hard they try to be holy, sin is always with them. If they let down their guard for just one moment, anger and lust leap in and overpower them. And Scripture seemingly confirms their experience. They know with Jeremiah that "the heart is deceitful above all things and beyond cure" (17:9). They have proved, with Paul, that "nothing good lives in [them], that is, in [their] sinful nature" (Rom. 7:18). They feel that God was surely talking about them when He said that "every inclination of the thoughts of [man's] heart was only evil all the time" (Gen. 6:5). And they can appeal to those passages that depict the behavior of different people of God when they catch a glimpse of the divine Majesty. Job says, "My eyes have seen you. Therefore I despise myself and repent in dust and ashes" (42:5–6). Isaiah says, "Woe to me . . . I am ruined! For I am a man of unclean lips, and I live among a people of unclean lips, and my eyes have seen the King, the LORD Almighty" (6:5). Daniel falls flat on his face when he sees the great vision and his radiant appearance is fearfully changed (10:8). John, when he sees the risen Christ in all His glory, falls at Jesus' feet as though dead (Rev. 1:17). Both Scripture and experience seem to force self-haters to take a negative view of themselves. This, in their view, is what it means to be human.

Furthermore, since our basic nature is so evil (according to our view), God is necessarily against everything that we really are. He has to put the "real me" to death. He has to bring me down to absolute zero so that I can be nothing and He can be all. In fact, only when He has so reduced me can His Spirit come into my life and use me. Then once He has come in, He can manipulate me as a hand manipulates a glove. And I, at last, will be able to please Him, for I will be rid of the wretched self that keeps getting in His way.

This view of human selfhood is what I call the "worm stance" or "worm theology." And, unfortunately, there's just enough truth amid the distortions to make it convincing to those who are susceptible to such a view of themselves; for Scripture does indeed teach that we are tragically prone to sin, and that we have been fearfully, even mortally, damaged by it. It teaches, too, that God is utterly against this sin in us and that He will go to any length to root it out. And it's true that there is something in all of us that needs to be mortified or put to death.

But in no sense is God against our essential nature. Sinful though we are, we are still not worms in His sight. We may indeed feel terribly worm-like when we catch a glimpse of the majesty and holiness of God—just as the saints did in Scripture. But we can be encouraged by the fact that God does not look upon us with the same contempt that we focus upon ourselves. Note, for example, that Job, in his worm experience, utterly despises himself, but God turns and praises him to his friends (Job 42:7–8). Similarly, Isaiah reaches a point where is he appalled at himself and his uncleanness, but God cleanses him and commissions him to His own service (Isa. 6:7–9). Daniel falls flat on his face in self-abasement before God, but God tells him that he is "highly esteemed" ("greatly beloved" RSV) and urges him to stand up (Dan. 10:11). John falls down as if dead before the glory of Christ, but the risen Lord says reassuringly, "Do not be afraid" (Rev. 1:17). Always God lifts His servants from their self-contempt and frees them from their fear.

Obviously, then, we are not worms in His sight; we are creatures of His own making and precious beyond all imagining. We're not puppets to be animated by the divine hand; we're His sons and daughters. God is not trying to crush us and reduce us to zero; He is seeking to make us in our very own selves—even in our unguarded moments— more and more like Himself in holiness, love, and wisdom. Indeed, we are special to Him, even in our fallen state before we become Christians. We are much more than worms to Him.

There are, however, many Christians, who, for one reason or another, are prone to this low view of themselves, who lack a sense of self-worth, who tend to hate themselves because of their sins and inadequacies. Such people can really believe in God's love only when everything is going well in their inner lives: when they sense sweet fellowship with God, when they have victory over their besetting sins, when they feel wholly yielded to God. But when something ruffles their inner calm or shows them to be in need of grace, they fall back on the old self-hatred. They decide they don't have the combination after all. They still don't know how to yield wholly to God. As they always knew, there is nothing good in them. So they keep on and on trying to negate them- selves. The sad part of it all is that they think God is doing

the same thing to them. He is trying, they feel, to reduce
them to absolute zero so He can take over.

The heart of the problem is this: Such people (and I was
one of them for many years) feel that the evil in them is the
essential self and the good is not. Any good is only God in
them. They think Paul's statement that "nothing good lives
in me, that is, in my sinful nature" (Rom. 7:18) refers to the
whole person, whereas Paul makes it clear that this worthlessness "is no longer I myself . . . but it is sin living in me"
(v. 17). He adds, furthermore, that in his inmost self he
delights in the law of God (v. 22). Actually, then, these self-
haters have the whole picture reversed. They think that the
evil is the "real me," and the good is not; but Paul, in effect,
says the exact opposite.

Given this attitude toward their essential nature, it is
impossible for self-haters to make very much out of the
grace of God. The only time God can possibly be sensed as
gracious is when they are groveling at His feet, reduced to
nothing, when there is absolutely no "me" left and He's
taken over everything. At any other time, grace is impossible.

TWO ASPECTS OF HUMAN NATURE

Since this worm view of human nature is so prevalent in
certain Christian circles, I must explain in more detail what I
understand the Bible to teach. First of all, let me say that
Scripture has two main emphases in talking about us: first,
that we are made in the image of God; and, second, that that
image is marred by sin. We call this latter emphasis the Fall,
a reference to Adam's falling away from God when he
sinned (see Gen. 3). Unless both aspects of our nature are
understood, we wind up with a distorted view. If, for
example, we focus exclusively upon mankind as made in the
image of God, we then come up with a sort of sweetness-
and-light view of our basic nature that minimizes the
seriousness of sin and renders Calvary unnecessary. But if
we focus exclusively on ourselves as fallen, we lose sight of
the glory of the mature humanness to which redemption

calls us. The first of these distortions—the sweetness-and-light view—has, I trust, been dealt with sufficiently in my earlier discussion of human sinfulness. I now consider the second.

SCRIPTURAL TEACHING ON THE IMAGE OF GOD

Scripture has this dual emphasis: mankind as made in the image of God and mankind as fallen. It's worth noting further that the Fall is the later development. Primarily, and first of all, man was made in God's image. Then afterward came the distortion of sin. This means that, if we could somehow undo the distortion, we would find behind and beneath it all something beautiful and godlike that the Lord Himself created—something beautiful and godlike not merely in terms of the qualities and rationality and creativity but more especially in terms of moral worth and the capacity to love.

This fact that we are made in the image of God is therefore still (despite the Fall) something fundamental to all of God's purposes in and for us. For example, in Genesis we read that after the Flood, God forbade murder because man had been made in the image of God (9:6). In other words, the fact that man is made in God's image renders human life of compelling value even after the Fall. James makes a similar point in his letter when he rebukes people for blessing God at one time and later with the same mouth cursing them. His reason is that people are made in the likeness of God (3:9). Man, then, is not a worm. He's not worthless. Even in his fallen state God demands that he be treated with respect.

Another clue to the significance of the image of God in man is found in the psalmist's description of the blessedness of children. They are described as a "heritage from the LORD" and a "reward" (127:3). They are "arrows in the hands of a warrior" (v. 4). "Blessed is the man whose quiver is full of them" (v. 5). Obviously, here Scripture regards children as good, desirable, and a gift from God.

Certainly, children are fallen just like the rest of us, but they still bear some of the loveliness of heaven about them. Sin has not blotted out all their beauty. Who that has been loved by a child can doubt it?

Still another evidence of the residual image of God in man can be seen from the way Jesus treated people. He was never repelled by human beings in their squalor and sin. He knew the deadly consequences of sin. He knew the necessity of final judgment. He knew that sin must eventually be put away. Yet He continually mingled freely with sinners. He did not find them repulsive. In fact, Jesus clearly appreciated and respected them as human beings. It is evident that He appreciated some sinners (the tax collectors and the harlots) more than others (the scribes and the Pharisees), which is to say that He saw the former had been less corrupted. There was more of the image of God still visible in them. By the same token, there was enough moral truth in their hearts that when they saw Jesus they could tell that He came from regions of greater moral beauty and purity than they. They could recognize the divine beauty when they saw it. This would have been impossible had they been totally corrupt, wholly depraved. In other words, they were fallen—but not beyond redemption. Love could touch them and bring them back to their true manhood and womanhood. Grace could reawaken what God had first created—distorted and crushed though it was.

THE IMAGE OF GOD IN EXPERIENCE

Experience teaches us the same thing that Scripture does. Man is indeed fallen, and there is no part of his nature that has been left unscathed by the deadly effects of sin. Yet everywhere we can still see the traces of the beauty that God created. There's still some sweetness left, some bits of innocence, some traces of genuine kindness, some trust, some self-giving love. Even the pale, distorted glimpses of the divine nature that we see in others are still beautiful.

We could also look at the problem in another way. If it were true that unregenerate man is totally corrupt, what

could we say about the genuine though imperfect love that
men and women sometimes display? We would have to
assume that it was all a fraud—all a front. That is, in fact,
what I myself once thought. I remember, for example, how
baffled I was one time when I read a moving story about a
truly compassionate teacher in a boarding school. There was
not the slightest evidence that she was a Christian, yet she
showed more genuine love for the children than I, a believer,
ever thought of having for anyone. She understood their
problems. She cared. And she gave herself for them in a way
that could only be called Christlike. "How could this be?" I
asked myself. "Unsaved people are supposed to be totally
fallen. They're not supposed to be able to love like this
unless they're born again." But this woman could and did.
And if we have eyes to see and hearts to understand, we have
to say that others also can and do.

If we are going to reach others for Christ, we have to
recognize the image of God in them. We may wish to
attribute that goodness in them to prevenient grace, as the
theologians call it, that gift of God that draws them even in
their sinfulness to Himself. Or we may credit the gracious
wooing of the Holy Spirit. But the goodness is there, call it
what we will.

In fact, people see and appreciate the beauty of Christ
only because they already have tasted and understood a copy
of that beauty in people. Because they themselves have been
made in the image of God and have lived with others made
in that image, they can begin to see some of the beauty of the
Lord our God in the face of Jesus Christ.

THE CORRUPTION OF THE IMAGE OF GOD

However, let it not be thought that, in emphasizing the
importance of the image of God in man, I therefore
minimize the fact and importance of the Fall. It's precisely
because we are made in the image of God that sin is such a
terrible thing, and it has corrupted something that God made
beautiful. There is no part of me that remains unaffected.
My will, my mind, my motives, my feelings, even my body

have suffered. Apart from divine aid, I have no hope of undoing the damage. Self-interest and deceit have entered my very bones. After a lifetime of effort, they will still be there. I am like a beast in a trap. I was created to roam free, but sin has snapped its jaws around me and imprisoned me. I am like an eagle with a broken wing. God intended that I should fly, soar high in the blue sky. But sin has broken me, and I cannot even get off the ground. I'm like a priceless violin created by a master. But the strings are broken, and the pegs slip, and the wood is cracked. When the master tries to play me, he gets nothing from me but discordant squawks.

FREEING THE IMAGE OF GOD

But, thank God, Jesus came to do something about my sin. He came to free the trapped animal, heal the broken wing, restore the discarded violin. He came to set me free from the prison in which sin has bound me. He came to release the real me, that which was made in the image of God, so that I can be what He created me to be. In the final analysis, God is not killing something evil (although there is that in me that needs to be killed); He is not corraling something wild (though there is that which needs controlling). He's freeing something bound, and "if the Son sets you free, you will be free indeed" (John 8:36). This is what God is in the business of doing. And it's His grace that does it:

> Down in the human heart, crushed by the tempter,
>   Feelings lie buried that grace can restore;
> Touched by a loving heart, wakened by kindness,
>   Chords that were broken will vibrate once more.
>   Fanny Crosby

TWO KINDS OF SELFHOOD

Now if God is, indeed, in the freeing rather than the killing business, where does the killing come in? Paul, for example, talks about putting to death the deeds of the body (Rom. 8:13). To explain, I should like to discuss the two aspects of human nature (the God-given and the sinful) from a different point of view. I should like to describe them in terms of two kinds of self or selfhood. There is one kind of self that, as I suggested earlier, lives in a one-self universe. Let's call this kind of self *the closed self.* The other kind of self lives in a universe where not only it, but all other selves, are intrinsically valuable. This kind of self is open, self-giving, secure, loving. Let's call this self *the open self*. Now the open self is precisely what God intended all selves to be when He created them. The open self exemplifies what it means to be made in the image of God. This is what God created us to be but what we no longer are. The closed self, on the other hand, is the essence of sin. It is the fallen self. Every man, woman, and child is now moving in its orbit. Every human being is tainted with its point of view. Not all are equally badly tainted, but all will be destroyed by its power in the end if they are not redeemed and if the corrupting power of sin is not stopped.

THE CLOSED SELF

As I suggested earlier, the closed self is basically at enmity with all other selves. Since the one self is all-important, all others are necessarily either actual or potential enemies. If their wishes and plans happen to coincide with its own, well and good. But if not, it must get preference. And it's beyond reason that its wishes and theirs should always correspond. So the weak are its lawful prey, and the strong constitute an inevitable threat to its welfare. God, of all selves, has to be the ultimate threat. Ultimately, He cannot be defeated, He cannot be fooled, and He cannot be avoided. He can only be hated.

THE LIE ABOUT GOD

It's important to see that the closed self's view of selfhood is essentially a lie. It's a falsehood from beginning

to end. First of all, it's based on a lie about God. When Eve
in the Garden of Eden tells the serpent about God's
command against eating the fruit of the tree under threat of
death, the serpent replies, "You will not surely die . . . For
God knows that when you eat of it your eyes will be opened,
and you will be like God, knowing good and evil" (Gen.
3:4–5). The serpent gives the lie to the trustworthiness and
goodness of God, for God cannot be fully trusted with
Adam and Eve's welfare. If they want the best, they are
going to have to look out for themselves. They have to look
out for Number One.

Then the product of the lie is unbelief, lack of trust. If
Adam and Eve had continued to trust God in the face of
temptation, there would have been no fall. But they could
not. At least, they did not. And with the first whisper of lack
of trust, the closed self was born. Hence, always, at the core
of the closed self is the big lie with its offspring—lack of
trust. Is it any wonder that the New Testament makes so
much of faith? Always it is the crucial issue. When the Holy
Spirit comes, He convinces the world of sin, not because of
all the wicked things people do, but because they do not
believe (John 16:8–9). When faith is missing, spiritual
disintegration follows. So on the heels of Adam and Eve's
unbelief come disobedience, fear, the hiding from God, the
passing of blame on to others, and, finally, the whole catalog
of human wickedness.

THE LIE ABOUT OTHER SELVES

The first lie, the first unbelief, was above all a matter
between the self and God. But the lie also includes all other
selves. They also are not to be trusted. Trust them and you
become vulnerable. They might take advantage of you.
They might hurt you. They might even destroy you.
Unfortunately, mixed in with the lie is more than a grain of
truth. Other people do take advantage of us. They do hurt
us and sometimes they even destroy us. The lie consists in
the belief that enmity is therefore the only alternative, that
love and trust are meaningless, that the only way to live is to

look out for one's self. But in truth there is an alternative. Love is not meaningless. Even on this sin-cursed earth love makes life richer, fuller, and freer. True, it may at times lead even to crucifixion, but it also leads to redemption. There is nothing like it, whether in this world or the world to come. But the big lie blinds us to the glory of the meaning of love.

THE LIE AGAINST ONESELF

The closed self is also a lie of yet another kind. It is a lie against one's own self. It is a falsehood against the very self that God created. In a sense it makes a self a non-self. What do I mean? Simply that God made us to operate on the fuel of love. We achieve our true selfhood only as we love one another. But when love and trust are gone, we have to erect a false self to protect ourselves. Some of us put on a belligerent self. We fight. We bully. We put other people down. But the real self, the self made to love, never has a chance to grow. Others of us hide. We make sure that no one ever gets close to us. No hint of the real self ever shows through. And so the real self shrivels. Still others of us put on the compliant "nice guy" act. We diligently keep doing what others expect us to do. But it's all a fraud, and we're not acting from the heart.

But whatever we do—whether we fight, hide, or comply—the result is the same. The real self cannot grow. The person whom God created cannot be himself or herself but remains imprisoned behind the false self that sin has created. It's the old story. I've tried to save my life, and I've lost it. I've tried to preserve a lonely, insecure self, and I've wound up with a non-self, a lie, a front, a fraud. I've eaten of the fruit of the tree that was supposed to make me become like God and I've died. And so have we all. This is the lie and the fruit of the lie that the father of lies has foisted off on us.

OUT OF THE FALSE SELF AND
INTO THE TRUE

Now we're ready to come back to the self-mortification that Paul talks about. It's this closed self, the false self, that has to die. In fact, in one sense, it is dead already, for nonlove is nonlife. But in another sense it is very much alive and dominates much of what we do. And it has to die. We have to move out of the old self and into the new, out of the lie and into the truth, out of the false me and into the real me—the me that God created. As Paul puts it, we need to "put off the old nature with its practices . . . [and] put on the new nature, which is being renewed in knowledge after the image of its creator" (Col. 3:9–10 RSV).

Only grace can enable us to do this. Grace tells us that even though we have sinned, even though we deserve to suffer the consequences of our sins, yet God accepts us and loves us as we are. Grace, then, destroys the lie about God. God is *not* Enemy Number One. He does not have it in for us. He's not out to destroy us. Instead, He's totally for us. We are reconciled to Him through the grace of our Lord. He loves us. He wants to free us. He wants to make us His sons and daughters. And when with the eyes of our spiritual understanding we see His grace, when we see Him for what He is, the old lie dies. The old mistrust melts. Faith is born and we can open our hearts to Him in a free response to the love He first gave us so freely. As we believe, the new self is born—the new person, the new nature, the open self that begins to know what it means to love God with all the heart, and to love one's neighbor as oneself. This is what God is doing in and for us. And it's His grace that does it.

NEW DIGNITY AND RESPONSIBILITY

The implications of all this are immense. If God in grace is freeing the "real me" in the way I have suggested, if He is affirming my selfhood, my personhood in this manner, then He is conferring upon me both a dignity and a responsibility beyond my wildest dreams.

One might have thought that grace would imply the exact opposite. After all, God, in His sovereign power and loving grace, did for us what we could never have done for ourselves, for we could not save ourselves. Our salvation is not of works. We contributed nothing to it. We have nothing to boast of. It was all God's doing. Our part was merely that of paupers accepting a free gift. And so mankind would appear to have been reduced to nothing at all.

Yet as we have seen, God is not in the business of negating human personality or selfhood. He does indeed crush the arrogance and self-sufficiency of the false self that sin has erected. But the real me, the self created by God, is His priceless treasure. I was even worth sending His Son to die for. There's not a single part of me that He does not prize. God has a special purpose for me. By His grace He is going to bring all the parts of my makeup together into a harmonious whole, and awaken what He created so that I can become the beautiful being He created me to be.

Since this is so, it becomes clear that God is not reducing human dignity and responsibility, but affirming it. One Man, Jesus, has shown us what God's purposes for us are; and because He has gone before, we may now follow Him. This is precisely the thought expressed by the writer of the letter to the Hebrews (2:5–9). According to him, God promised mankind glory and honor, but this promise has so far been fulfilled only in the person of Christ. So He is our forerunner, the first to receive the inheritance promised to us all. Because of Him we can come to full manhood, mature womanhood.

If God were trying to destroy the "real me" as sinful, and substitute His Spirit in its place—or if He were trying to reduce me to nothing in a divine takeover—then we could talk about reduction of human dignity and responsibility. I'm not sure how we could reconcile such intentions with any gracious purpose on God's part, but it seems clear that individual selfhood would be of importance only as something to be negated.

But this is not what God is trying to do. He's not trying to reduce us to nothing; He's trying to make us *something*—something beautiful, something special. He wants to help us by grace to become each in our own unique way like Christ, to become the kind of people who know and understand God's will, who love that will, and actively choose it because we love it. He wants to make us into the kind of people He doesn't have to dominate moment by moment, doesn't have to keep handing out orders to, doesn't have to override.

In other words, we are not puppets dancing to the divine Puppeteer. We are not gloves animated by the divine hand. We are not tools or instruments used by the divine Master Craftsman. Rather, we are stewards to whom God turns over the responsibility of managing His property and carrying out His purposes. It's up to us to use our gifts, our wisdom, our commitment in His service. We are mature sons and daughters no longer under rules, no longer under tutors and governors (Gal. 3:23–4:5). We have come into our inheritance, and that inheritance is now ours to manage. In our own hearts we are acquiring the divine love and the divine wisdom. We are becoming tuned to the divine purpose, and His concerns are becoming our own. God's laws are being written on our hearts, and a whole new world of dignity and responsibility is now ours.

8 | LEARNING TO CHOOSE WISELY

As we have seen, grace means responsibility. Put another way, when God takes the reins of my life, He does not take those reins out of my hands. In fact, He puts them into my hands in a way that would have been neither useful nor safe apart from grace. As He changes me, as He writes His law upon my heart, He is making me into the kind of person He can trust. He therefore leaves it up to me to take responsibility and to do His will from the heart.

If grace means responsibility, then responsibility means—among other things—making God-centered, God-honoring decisions. In other words, the decisions *are* ours to make, and these decisions fill our lives. How shall we use our time from day to day? How shall we use our money? How shall we use our leisure? What kind of commitments should we make to the church? How much time should we devote to our families? What service shall we undertake for others? What kind of employment shall we choose? What kind of training should we get? Whom should we marry? Should we change jobs? Should we go into so-called Christian service? Decisions, decisions, decisions! Life is full of them, important and trivial, routine or life-changing. No one can escape them. They are ours to make whether we like it or not. And once made, they both reveal what we are and shape what we become. No one can either express or build the grace life without taking the responsibility for making the kinds of decisions that are pleasing to God.

The next question, then, is this: How do we know what God wants of us in any given situation? How do we learn to make those decisions that always please Him? How do we discover God's will in all the multiplicity of life's decisions? These are questions that have been asked by sincere Christians since time immemorial.

I must confess that I myself have spent a great deal of time and effort both in asking and answering such questions. But more recently I have come to the conclusion that an enormous proportion of this time and effort on my part, and on the part of many, many others, has been directed at trying to get God to do something for us that ordinarily He does not intend to do. We want Him to tell us what to do in a given situation. But God would rather confront us with the principles and commands He has already provided in Scripture and elsewhere and leave the decision up to us. We want Him to make our decisions for us so that we can avoid the risk of making mistakes and come up with the perfect, infallible decisions that only God can make. Yet it is God's will for us to remain ordinary human beings who make fallible decisions and learn wisdom and commitment by our mistakes. We want Him to take responsibility for our decisions, but He hands that responsibility back to us so that as we accept that responsibility we can grow into full maturity as His sons and daughters.

DIRECTION VERSUS WISDOM

Perhaps I can make the issue a little clearer if I attempt to describe two different approaches to the problem of making God-honoring decisions. One approach I call the *direction method* and the other the *wisdom method*.

In the direction method, one tries to make the right decision by obtaining directions or orders from God. It is assumed that God has something like a blueprint for every Christian—a perfect plan that includes a divinely ordained decision at every turn of the road. The duty of the Christian, then, is to avoid any independent decisions, and at every point to seek and find that perfect plan, that perfect decision from God, and then to do what He says without asking questions and without any back talk. All decisions should come from headquarters. One should therefore avoid the kind of self-will in which one makes one's own plans, and then tries to sanctify them by adding, "If it be Thy will." Instead, one should find out God's will before making the decisions and then act accordingly. It is assumed, furthermore, that God is as eager to communicate His will in any given matter as we are to find it. He may speak to us through Scripture or through sanctified common sense or through any one of a wide variety of ways. But it is usually necessary to wait for the still small voice of the Holy Spirit to give the final assurance in our hearts. If the voice speaks, all the experience or wisdom in the world should not turn us from the indicated path. If it does not, we have no right to move forward.

In the wisdom method, on the other hand, the Christian goes to God for *wisdom* rather than for *direction*. He seeks to know and understand the principles that God lays out in Scripture, prayerfully uses the wisdom God supplies, arrives at the best course of action he can devise, and then acts. This is not to rule out God's direction altogether. God is sovereign, and He can, at any time He chooses, step into our lives and tell us, "Do this!" or, "Do that!" But ordinarily He does not. Even in the more important things such as marriage or vocation, He doesn't give us very explicit guidance. He merely asks us to do all to the glory of God, and leaves us to determine, under the authority of Scripture, what doing all to the glory of God will mean in any given situation. In other words, in most of the decisions of life, God simply asks us to use our sanctified, biblically informed common sense. This is what I mean by the wisdom method.

It will already be clear to the reader that I am opting for the wisdom method of making Christian decisions as opposed to the direction method. I repeat, however, that I am not ruling out divine direction in the decision-making process. At any time God may step into our lives and tell us to do something that He wants done. For example, He told Moses from the burning bush in the wilderness, "Go. I am sending you to Pharaoh to bring my people the Israelites out of Egypt" (Ex. 3:10). He told Gideon at the threshing floor, "Go in the strength you have and save Israel out of Midian's hand. Am I not sending you?" (Judg. 6:14). He forbids Paul to preach the gospel in Asia or Bithynia, and then in a vision instructs Paul to take the gospel to Macedonia (Acts 16:6–10). Clearly, then, God sometimes does tell us explicitly what to do in a given situation. Furthermore, when He speaks, we have no option but to obey—none, that is if we wish to continue to enjoy His blessing in our lives.

I am not saying, then, that God never directs, never hands down a ready-made decision, never tells us specifically what to do. But He usually doesn't. This may sound terribly unspiritual and mundane, but God is often much more mundane than we would like Him to be. He *can* do the spectacular thing, but He usually doesn't. He *can* feed the hungry with food brought by ravens from heaven as He did for Elijah, but usually He expects us to go out and provide for our daily food by working with our hands. He *can* heal the sick, but He usually expects us to take responsibility for our own health—through proper food, exercise, rest, and medical care. (Interestingly, when God does give explicit direction in Scripture, it almost always comes unsought. It is not the product of anxious hours of prayer for guidance; it comes rather from God's sovereign choice, unasked for, unexpected, and often even unwanted.) All that He promises us is wisdom. Then it's up to us to decide what course of action He would most likely prefer at any given fork in the road, and then to act accordingly. He doesn't usually say to us, "Take this job"; "Go to that school." Instead, He says, "Here are the Scriptures, full of principles applicable to your daily life; apply them the best you know how to the present situation."

THE WISDOM METHOD AND SCRIPTURE

The Bible has much to say about God's purposes for us, but it is important to see that the emphasis seems to be placed primarily on His *general* purposes for each one of us.

These purposes are spoken of in terms of our relationship to Christ (John 6:40; Acts 22:14), the necessity for holy living (Eph. 1:4; 1 Thess. 4:3), and the Christian's commission to service through the exercise of his gifts (Rom. 12:1–8). Never are there any instructions for finding God's direction or for making the "correct" decision. In other words, if we want to pattern our lives after the direction method, we have no clear instructions to guide us, but if we want to use the wisdom method the whole Bible lights our way. Scripture is full of principles and teachings to enable us to become wiser about God's purposes and ways so that we can learn to make the kind of decisions that please Him.

The key to the problem of making God-honoring decisions may perhaps be found in the principle of stewardship. Remember the story Jesus told of the master who gave out the sums of money to each of his servants, with the expectation that each should make the most of what he had received (Matt. 25:14–30). Evidently no detailed instructions or advice was offered as to how to proceed. It was up to the servants whether they were to work in cattle, sheep, grapes, wheat, or in other business. They all took responsibility, did the best they could, and were rewarded for their diligence and faithfulness. All, that is, except one. He did not dare to make a mistake, for what would the master say if he decided wrong? So he hid his sum of money and returned it to his master unused. It was he and he alone who earned his master's anger, and that was because he refused to take responsibility for using what the master gave him. He would not take the risk of choosing on his own.

As Christians we follow the example of this man only at our peril. God has given us gifts to use for Him, and it's up to us to use them. We cannot wait for the Voice from heaven. We must start moving for Him, serving Him, using our gifts for Him, giving our lives for Him in the best way that we know. At any time God may step in with other orders; meantime, we must do our utmost to use what He has given us in His service. God cannot, as the old saying goes, steer a ship that is dead in the water.

THE WISDOM METHOD AND EXPERIENCE

Not only Scripture, but experience, teaches us that decisions must be made on the wisdom basis. We know, for example, what happens to a child if his parents make all his decisions for him. A part of him is destroyed. He becomes stunted and warped, unable to choose and act as a mature human being. This is so not merely because parents are fallible and frequently make wrong decisions for the child. Even if every decision they made was right, the child would still suffer. Their rightness would make it even worse. After all, if they were wrong part of the time, the child could then have some excuse for asserting himself and making a few decisions of his own. But if they are always right—never.

To put it another way, God is willing to let us make mistakes—sometimes even disastrous ones—if only we can learn from them. He knows very well that all of us acquire ninety percent of our wisdom by the trial-and-error method. So He gives us responsibility and lets us make our own mistakes. He is not overly concerned, at this stage in our lives, that we should always be right. Few of us can bear the burden of infallibility, especially if it purports to come to us from God.

And who has not seen some of the errors and excesses committed by those who have mistakenly convinced themselves that God has told them what to do? There is, for example, the arrogant, self-assured person who tries to foist off onto others decisions supposedly from God that everyone around him knows come from his own desires. (Perhaps the reader has heard the story of the man who informed a young lady that God had told him she was to be his wife. He received the very sensible reply, "Well, God hasn't told *me* yet.") Then there's the timid soul who finds himself saddled with an unsatisfying vocation simply because he feels that it is God's will. In actual fact he has made a mistake, but he can't learn from that mistake because he feels he is doing what God told him to do. So he's stuck with it. Then there is the passive, self-doubting Christian who never learns to take risks or strike out on his own. He has to wait till he hears the voice of God before he can make any important move, but he never hears that voice. Or if he hears it, he no sooner begins to act than he begins to fear his decision is wrong; so he vacillates painfully back and forth, never quite able to make up his mind. Or perhaps it turns out (without his ever realizing it) that the voice he thinks he hears always expresses the wishes of those Christians nearest to him who, he thinks, are stronger or wiser than he.

If we wait for God to tell us what to do, we develop a passive Christianity. We content ourselves with the idea that we are doing what we are told and are therefore pleasing God. But God wants more than passive obedience. He wants active, choosing, outgoing love and service. Our commitment is not to be measured by whether we are prepared to say yes to all the explicit demands God makes of us. It is to be measured by our willingness to throw our whole being into holy living and into giving ourselves for the sake of suffering humanity—by our willingness to make and go on making the kind of decisions that reflect this total abandonment to the will of God. Our decisions must not be merely those that God dishes out (though when He speaks, we must obey); they must be an expression of a mind that knows and understands something of God's purposes and of a heart in love with those purposes—sold out to the love of Christ for dying men and women, and ready to do all in its power to express that love.

PRINCIPLES GOVERNING WISE DECISIONS

Grace motivation. If we are to make wise, God-honoring decisions, we need to learn to make choices that proceed from and result in grace-motivated obedience and service. If our decisions, our commitments, our service, our obedience to God proceed only from a sense of duty or from a necessity to obey a God who is always wiser and stronger than we are, we are of all people most miserable. Such obedience is worthless. It pleases neither God nor others. Nor does it please ourselves. It is of the flesh, and it can only destroy us. In the end our lives will prove nothing but a fraud. It may even lead us to the point where the Christian life becomes a burden and where God Himself becomes hateful. Obedience that does not spring from the gracious love of God and our response to that love is little better than trash.

Yet here we face a dilemma. Most of us have pitifully little grace motivation in us. In fact it is doubtful whether any of us is ever motivated *wholly* by the love that grace produces. There is always a root of selfishness, obligation, or necessity driving us on. If before doing anything we were to wait until we *felt* like serving God, or until a warm glow of love suffused us, many of us would scarcely ever get started. What are we to do?

My suggestion is this: In facing a given commitment or decision, we should not worry too much about the present state of our motivation—whether it is good, bad, or indifferent. Rather, we should be concerned with whether the commitment will lead to growth in our capacity to love and serve God truly. We should not ask, "Am I acting wholly from grace motivation?" but, "Will my action produce growth in grace?" It is, of course, true that sometimes we have to commit ourselves to a course of action that drains our motivation. In such a case we have to consider seriously whether we have the resources to undertake the commitment in question. No one can survive for long in a situation where the spiritual outflow is greater than the intake. Sooner or later we'll find ourselves doing more harm than good in the course of action we have embarked upon.

This means that time, experience, and a certain amount of self-knowledge are always ingredients in the process of learning to make increasingly grace-motivated commitments. For example, if I am confronted with the challenge to teach a Sunday school class or to spend an hour every day in prayer, I have to ask myself, "Is this commitment likely, in the long run, to lead to increased joy in serving God, increased spiritual strength, greater genuineness, more love for God and people? If I don't know the answer, I may try it out for a while—a good, solid, genuine trial—to see what the results are. I may then find the Sunday school class a challenge. The further I go, the more rewarding and worthwhile it gets. The new schedule of prayer may turn out to be demanding but spiritually strengthening and worth the effort. But things may turn out just the opposite. The class may prove to be nothing but a drain. It may become more and more burdensome with the passage of time. The times of prayer may be self-defeating because they are more than I can handle. The longer I stay with the commitment, the more hateful it becomes—not building my fellowship with God but destroying it. But whether the commitment in question builds me up or tears me down I have learned something about myself; I know something more about the kind of commitments I need to make or to avoid making.

If we commit ourselves to the kind of decisions that do in fact lead to growth in grace and to increased grace motivation, we will find that we are always stretching. If we are really growing, we can never remain satisfied today with the level of service and commitment that we attained yesterday. God always has something more, something better, something more challenging, something more rewarding for us to do than we have been able to manage hitherto. This something more will not be something way beyond us or something that will overburden us, but it will keep us from settling for the status quo. God will never let us get into a rut. He will never let us be content with a nice, easy, undemanding life. He wants us always to be growing, reaching beyond where we are. We can all become better and more effective than we now are. Our grace-growth decisions and commitments should make this possible. We need to keep stretching.

Submission to Christ's lordship. Another principle that should govern our decisions is that of submission to the lordship of Christ. This means a personal covenant with Him, acknowledging Him as Lord and Master—a covenant that is daily renewed throughout one's life. It means obedience to the express commands of Christ for holy living as laid down in Scripture. It means commitment to the service of God and man. It means accepting and welcoming

His providences—the joys, sorrows, limitations, and opportunities that He chooses to send into our lives.

Any denial of Christ's lordship is always destructive of the grace life. If, for example, we knowingly and deliberately disobey an explicit command of Christ, our grace motivation is necessarily destroyed. We cannot at the same time respond joyfully to the love of God and also deliberately flout His commands. It's not that God ceases to love us or that He is no longer gracious. It's that we've chosen to operate on another principle. We've deliberately closed our eyes to that grace and acted as if it were irrelevant to the present situation.

Grace motivation is likewise undercut by any refusal to accept a given responsibility or commitment that the Lord sets before us. This includes anything from washing dirty dishes to the challenge of changing one's vocation. If we balk at the decision or commitment, our general motivation and spiritual well-being begin to suffer. We begin to labor under a sense of guilt. We lose our self-respect and even begin to feel that God is nagging and condemning us. In actual fact He is not. He understands the doubts and fears that hold us back, and He is standing beside us to help, waiting to transform our lives from drudgery to joy, from fear to confidence, and from burdensomeness to glad service. But the longer we balk, the harder it is to see God's grace and respond to it. It does no good to hold back.

We lose out also if our decisions and commitments fail to reflect a willing recognition of God's sovereign providence. In other words, we cannot ignore or rebel against His right to manage our lives and our circumstances as He sees fit. James, for example, rebukes those who make plans entirely on their own without reference to God's providential will. They say, "Today or tomorrow we will go to such and such a town and spend a year there trading and making money." Yet they "have no idea what tomorrow will bring." It has not occurred to them to think about what God has in store for them. What they ought to say, James tells us, is, "If it be the Lord's will, we shall live to do this or that" (4:13–15 NEB).

That is to say, we are free to go ahead and make plans as seems best to us, but we should always do so recognizing God's sovereign power over our lives—for sickness or for health, for life or for death. In the final analysis, we are not our own. It is not for us to have the final word. To think or act otherwise is to court disaster or to find ourselves over and over again at odds with God. Instead of a loving Father giving us what He thinks best, He becomes either a stranger whose plans and purposes are no concern of ours or an enemy who continually interferes in our lives, dashing our hopes and thwarting our plans. There is no grace in such a relationship with God—only emptiness or frustration. We have no alternative but to acknowledge His providence and welcome it as from the hands of One who has loved us with an everlasting love—One who is so totally for us that no power on earth or in hell can ever be successful against us. We need to acknowledge the lordship of Christ in this area of our lives.

Matching commitments to personal growth and gifts. Yet another principle that should guide us in our decision-making is that of matching our commitments to our spiritual growth and to our gifts. There seems to be a strong tendency among some Christians to want to make all kinds of extreme commitments, and then to justify them by appealing to the power of God to bring the desired results. (After all, Phil. 4:13 tells us we can do all things through Christ!) And if the results don't come about, we conclude that the cause is lack of faith and commitment on our part. Or perhaps we give up and decide that there isn't any point in trying to give ourselves to God's service. He doesn't do His part. It's almost as if we were to find a thousand-pound rock that must be moved out of the middle of the road, and then were to figure that if only we pray hard enough or have enough faith or exert enough effort, we ought to be able to pick it up with our bare hands and toss it over into the ditch. If we find that we can't, we feel that God has somehow let us down. In short, we act as if our present state of growth, our capacities, interests, preferences, personalities, and psychological limitations are all irrelevant to the problem of making decisions that please God. And this, of course, is nonsense.

The fact is that our commitments should match our point of growth, not only physically (that is obvious; you do not send a six-year-old to stack fifty-pound boxes) but also psychologically and spiritually. God does not ask children to do adults' work. Yet how often we Christians let ourselves fall into just this trap! We overreach ourselves and then wonder why things don't work out.

We need, then, to beware of overcommitment, for this always leads to trouble, to continual failure and frustration. You find yourself becoming more and more defeated in your attitude. The harder you try, the worse things get. You begin to hate the unrelenting demands that God seems to be making of you. You are in prison and you want out. Grace motivation has gone out the window, and there's nothing left but condemnation and guilt in its place.

Not only are you battling a sense of failure and defeat, but you have so little time or inclination to develop deep, loving relationships with anyone. As you feel the sense of failure and impotence, you pull away from other Christians. You are afraid they'll see through the hollowness of your life. And so one more means of grace is sacrificed, for grace knowledge and motivation are all but impossible apart from the reinforcement provided by deep, supportive fellowship with other Christians.

Perhaps worst of all is the fact that one has no time to call one's own. There's no time to relax. No time to enjoy oneself. No time for genuine spiritual refueling. Everything and everyone is important except oneself. Everyone's needs, desires, expectations, or hopes are met but one's own. One is unimportant. One is worthless. One is nothing.

But it's all unnecessary. God doesn't want us to undertake more than we can really handle. He doesn't want burdened, squirrel-cage service. He doesn't want us to labor under a load of failure, guilt, and worthlessness. He wants us to choose carefully how best we can serve Him with the spiritual power and energy that we now have. He wants us to be able to rejoice in His service. And He wants us to set the priorities and make the decisions that make all this possible. Then as we do, our power, energy, and joy will grow.

Our commitments should match not only our stage of growth, but also our natural and God-given capacities and gifts. Some people seem to think that God's will for them is necessarily going to be something nasty, something contrary to their natural inclinations, something that goes against the grain. It's true that the Christian life is going to make great demands upon us, to require discipline, to ask us to step beyond the world of our personal convenience and pleasure. But on the other hand, God made us the way we are for a purpose. Every bit of it is part of His goodwill. And He's not in the business of putting round pegs in square holes. He's given us all special capacities and gifts, and He wants us to use them. Even our likes and dislikes are a part of the pattern. They tell us something about the way God made us. Everything that He made He wants us to use for Him. So what we are—our gifts, abilities, personalities, preferences—all figure into God's purposes for us.

These principles are by no means the only ones to consider in arriving at God-honoring decisions. But for our present purposes only a brief mention of a few other principles will be sufficient.

Necessity. Some things simply have to be done whether we like it or not. Meals must be prepared, dishes washed, the garden tilled, the car repaired, and somehow we must find some way to make a living. We cannot escape these necessities, and there can be no happiness or fruitful service if we balk at our duties, resent them, or insist on running away from them. They simply have to be done.

Human need. Another principle is that of human need. People all around us need help; they're lonely, hungry, hurt. We cannot do everything, but we must do something. We must show the love Christ has for others by the way we care about their hurts and by the way we reach out to help.

Feasibility. Some courses of action are physically, psychologically, and spiritually feasible. Others are not, and God wants us to face the facts. Sometimes I think Christians are willing to be guided by physical feasibility but not by psychological. They won't try to build a fifty-thousand-dollar home with income from a four-dollar-an-hour job. They don't build a sink so that the water has to flow uphill in order to drain. But they are often willing to fly in the face of psychological or spiritual limitations merely by reciting the motto: *God can*, as if God no longer expects us to guide our behavior by the normal laws of cause and effect, which He wrote into the universe when He created it and us.

The trustworthiness of God. Another factor to be considered is God's power and trustworthiness. He can be expected to stand behind a valid faith commitment. We can afford to abandon the secure position and launch out upon an unknown path as Abraham did (Gen. 12), knowing that God will not let us down. It is safe to put God's interests ahead of our own because He promises that when we do He will look after our interests (Matt. 6:33).

Body orientation. The last principle I'll mention is that of body orientation. That is, our decisions often must be shared with other members of the body of Christ. This is especially true of those choices that involve our Christian vocation. Some matters are of such importance that we must not make up our minds about them by ourselves, even if on our knees before God. They should grow out of our life and service in the body of believers. For example, Paul and Barnabas embarked on their first missionary journey as a result of a group decision. It was to the *group* that the Holy Spirit said, "Set apart for me Barnabas and Saul for the work to which I have called them" (Acts 13:2).

Our ideal (by way of contrast) seems to be to spend enormous amounts of time trying to get God to tell us all by ourselves what to do. Then, after a crisis experience, we conclude that God has called us to Africa or India as missionaries. So we present ourselves to an agency to send us out. I suspect God would be more pleased if we would devote ourselves to service in and through His body where we are, and the whole body would see that we have been called to a wider service and together we'd pray and work toward carrying out the divine call. In short, Christian vocation is not strictly a Jesus-and-I proposition. It is an outgrowth of the life of the particular body of believers among whom we are serving Christ, and I'm not talking about so-called full-time Christian service. This principle is valid regardless of our vocation. We are to ask the believers with whom we worship to review what we sense God is telling us. By ourselves we can easily misread the mind of God and so we need the safeguard of others' judgment.

FACING THE TASK OF PROPERLY APPLYING THE PRINCIPLES

The above, then, are some of the principles that guide us in the various decisions of our lives. If you are anything like me, you may find it all overwhelming. Who is sufficient for these things? How can anyone weigh all these factors and come out with the truly wise, God-honoring decision? How, for example, does one know whether to launch out in faith on some new venture, or to "face facts" and conclude that the venture is unfeasible? How does one balance the competing claims of individual versus corporate guidance? How does one weigh one's own gifts and limitations against the needs of others? Surely only Omniscience is equal to such a task!

I must say that I can sympathize with the sense of inadequacy and even dismay that lie behind such questions. But I dare not make the task God has given us any easier than He has made it. True, only Omniscience can see all the factors involved in any decision that we make. Yet Omniscience has, in the main, chosen not to diminish us by doing the job for us. God seldom takes the easy way to train us, and I see no scriptural or practical reason for believing that He does so in this aspect of our lives. He sets before us the demanding yet infinitely worthwhile task of making these decisions ourselves, foolish and faithless though we often are. He chooses to let us struggle, fail, and struggle again so that in the process we may learn the meaning of true wisdom and true commitment. Every step of the way He is with us, here to encourage, there to close a door; here to shed some additional light, there to smooth the way. In another place, He will pick up the pieces if need be, deepening and enriching our lives by the experience.

ASKING FOR WISDOM

However, I remind you that God has promised wisdom to those who ask Him for it. "If any of you lacks wisdom," James says, "he should ask God, who gives generously to all without finding fault, and it will be given to him" (1:5). So we can seek for wisdom and find what we seek. God doesn't necessarily tell us exactly what to do in any particular situation, but if we diligently seek His face, He will give us the wisdom to understand the various factors involved and to perceive what principles may be applicable.

Perhaps I can best explain the way this works by telling you how a friend of mine once expressed it when another questioned him about his Christian life. "Does God tell you what to do when you have a problem?" he asked. My friend stopped and thought a moment, for he was a relatively new Christian and had never asked himself that before. Then he replied, "No, I guess God just turns on the light." That's what God does. He doesn't tell us what to do, but He does give us the kind of spiritual light that helps us to understand the issues involved in alternate courses of action. Then we ourselves can choose a way that honors Him.

DOING ONE'S BEST

Let me remind you, also, that God does not expect that we will unfailingly make the perfectly wise or correct decision at every moment. He does not demand instantaneous perfection in wisdom any more than in any other area of our lives; "he knows how we are formed, he remembers that we are dust" (Ps. 103:14). He does, however, demand that we attempt to make the wisest decision possible under the circumstances. He does ask that we do the best we can with the wisdom He has given us, whether that wisdom be the one-talent kind or the five-talent kind. We can trust His unfailing providence to undergird us in all that we do. This then is our part in the decision-making process, to do our best and trust God's providence.

I've said that God does not require instantaneous perfection in our decisions, but this does not mean that we should cease reaching toward perfection. Although we never achieve it in this life, yet we press on. We come as close to it as we can with the capabilities God has given us. This is what it means to do one's best.

Just so with our Christian decisions. God does not hold us responsible for making the one and only perfect decision at every turn of life's road. He asks us only to do the best we can. In the learning process we are bound to make many, many mistakes. But these need not be cause for dismay or discouragement, for, as we continue to take the responsibility of using to the full our modicum of spiritual wisdom, we grow in our ability to choose and to do those things that most please our Lord. In this area of our lives, then, as in all others, we simply have to accept our own imperfections, but keep growing, keep doing our best.

SECOND-GUESSING GOD'S PERFECT WILL

If we really do accept the fact that God gives us the responsibility to make our own decisions, even to the point of allowing us to make our own mistakes, we will be able to avoid another error that Christians often make: that of trying to second-guess what God's perfect decision may be in any given instance. There's a sense in which God's will for our lives includes every tiniest decision and turn in life's road. So even the most trivial act such as choosing which side of the street to walk on may prove to be a matter of immense importance in God's purposes for us. If we walk on the east side, we just might meet someone who would change the course of our whole lives. But if we walk down the west side, the new opportunity might be lost forever. Unforeseeable consequences such as this are simply not our concern. If God purposes that we shall meet that person on the east side of the street, He is able, if He so desires, to put into our hearts an unaccountable urge to cross the street. However, it seems much more likely that the crossing would take place as the result of what might strike us as sheer chance or even as the result of absentmindedness or stupidity on our part. God does not ask us to weigh imponderables or second-guess purposes of His that are beyond our foresight. We don't have to figure out ahead of time whether God wants us on this side of the street or that. We choose what seems best and leave the results to Him.

This may seem obvious enough when one thinks about minor decisions such as choosing which side of the street to walk on. But it is equally true, if less obvious, when it comes to more important matters such as choosing a vocation or a marriage partner. No one in his right mind can take such decisions lightly. They are fraught with all kinds of possibilities, some of which we can predict and some of which we can't. We can only do our best.

If we are confronted with a major decision, and we weigh all the factors as best as we know how (considering the various principles that I have suggested), and we conclude that either of two actions appears equally wise and honoring to God, then, so far as our responsibility is concerned, it doesn't matter which we choose. Obviously, the choice will have far-reaching consequences either way. But that's not our business. That's God's. If He sees that the decision is going in a direction that He in His wisdom knows is undesirable, He can be trusted to arrange a crucial "accidental" meeting or to send down a bolt from heaven or whatever. Our responsibility is simply to make the wisest choice we know. If the available options appear equal, which they probably never really are, and the choice simply must be made immediately, then there's no reason in the world why we should not go according to personal preference, follow a hunch, or even decide our course of action by the toss of a coin. The choice of one alternative over another in such a case is not a spiritual issue. We can simply go forward, even in the darkness of uncertainty, knowing that we are keeping faith with God, and that He will keep faith with us.

TRUSTING GOD'S PROVIDENCE

If this seems like a dangerous way to make decisions, it *is* dangerous. God has never been one to remove all the perils from the path that we take. Yet wherever our path may lead, we still can walk with confidence, for God's gracious, all-wise providence goes with us every step of the way. He may, indeed, leave almost all of life's decisions strictly up to us, yet He never leaves us alone in the process, and He can be counted on to respond to our decisions in the best way possible.

God may respond to our need, whether before or after our decision, by some definite direction of His own. For example, Paul decides to go into Bithynia, but the Spirit of Jesus forbids it. We are not told how. Then Paul has a dream in which a man from Macedonia appeals to him to go over to help them, and Paul concludes that God is calling him to go (Acts 16:7–10). Such direction may come for us in any of a variety of ways. Perhaps God will speak through a dream as He did to Paul, through an unshakable inner conviction, by giving a group of people an inescapable prayer burden, through a compelling linking together of circumstances, or through a phrase of Scripture taken out of context. But none of these means of direction should be *sought* after nor should any of them be taken, in and of themselves, as incontrovertible proof that God is leading. Very many people, I am sure, have experiences such as these that lead them to imagine God is directing when He is not. When God actually does direct, I suspect that His voice will be unmistakable. When God wants to get through to us, He will, and there will be no possibility of doubt as to what He wants.

But I say again that such explicit direction from God is not His usual way of operating. Usually His hand in our lives is much more subtle, even commonplace. He leaves us to make the choices that Christian responsibility requires; then, through His incomparable wisdom, certain ordinary-seeming things happen to us. A door opens here, another closes there. By chance we meet this person. By design we meet that one. By necessity, or perhaps lightheartedly, we make this or that particular decision. Afterward, when we look back on it all, it adds up to a pattern we could never have dreamed of ahead of time. We find that day after day, month after month, year after year God has directed us in ways utterly past our understanding. In the final analysis, as Jeremiah says, "Man's ways are not of his own choosing; nor is it for a man to determine his course in life" (10:23 NEB). We make the wisest decisions we can, but it is God who has the final say. And He makes no mistakes.

The most incredible part of it all is that ultimately even our mistakes fit into the pattern. Certain mistakes, in His infinite kindness, He aborts or blocks. Certain others, even very serious ones, He allows to bear their terrible fruit. This turns out to be a kindness. He knows that some of these worst mistakes spring from a radical defect deep down in our hearts, and that the defect will never be corrected unless we see it for what it is through the fruit that it bears. So He lets us fall flat on our faces. He lets us make a mess of things. He lets us lose precious months and even years of our lives. He allows the wounds to pierce deep, deep into our hearts. But when we come through on the other side, we find that God has done something in us and for us that we will be thankful for all our days. Out of folly and ugliness He has brought His own wisdom and beauty.

I know that this is true because God has done this very thing for me. Years ago when my wife and I first went to the mission field, we were sure that we were doing the right thing. As far as I could see, the whole of my life had pointed in that direction, and all my hopes and dreams were about to be fulfilled. I had no idea that spiritually and psychologically I was totally unfitted for the task I was undertaking. God could have blocked the door and kept me from going. But He didn't. He knew that I would learn more from total failure in Thailand than I could ever learn in any other way. If the defects in my spiritual life and psychological makeup were to be dealt with, I had to be put under the kind of pressure that forced me to see them for what they were. So God let me go out as a missionary. He let me fail. He let me reach the end of the road. He let me pass through several years of barrenness and emptiness where I could no longer serve Him or have fellowship with Him.

Yet all of this was the very best thing that could have happened to me. For through it and because of it I discovered things I had never really understood about God and His incomparable grace. Because of it I have a ministry for Christ I never could have had without it. God has given me "garlands instead of ashes, oil of gladness instead of mourners' tears, a garment of splendour for the heavy heart" (Isa. 61:3 NEB). I cannot thank Him enough for the seeming tragedy He allowed.

But that's the way God does things. Out of the ultimate folly and wickedness of Calvary, He brings the beauty and the cleansing of redemption. Out of man's weakness, He brings strength. Who would not trust the wise and loving providence of such a God?

9 | LEARNING TO ACCEPT AND EXPRESS FEELINGS

One of the great problem areas in allowing grace to function freely in our lives is the area of feelings. So many feelings can get us down: anger, lust, depression, resentment, jealousy, anxiety . . . The list is almost endless. These come and go, beyond our control, crushing, burning, shaking, shattering. Over and over again they make a mockery of our hard-won spirituality, our sweet, soul-refreshing peace with God. And in their wake come shame, self-condemnation, and a sense of baffled impotence. Why can't we get hold of ourselves? Why can't we get the victory? Why do we fail so often? And so we find ourselves shivering in the cold of our own failures, an almost infinite distance from the haven of God's grace and acceptance.

INDULGING FEELINGS

A large part of our difficulty results from jumping to the conclusion that only two things can be done with negative feelings: Either we indulge them or we squelch them. For the Christian, the first alternative seems to be ruled out. Jesus warns us in no uncertain words about the deadliness of anger and lust. Hardly a one of the negative emotions escapes rebuke from the Scriptures. How can we indulge these feelings and claim to be His sons and daughters? In fact not only does Scripture warn against such indulgence, but so do our own personal experiences. We've

all suffered at one time or another from people who have
vented their negative feelings upon us. The world is full of
those who have been deeply hurt by other people's anger,
lust, resentment, and the like. We've seen the destructiveness
of some of these feelings in our own hearts when we give
them free rein.

SUBDUING FEELINGS

Many of us have therefore concluded that these feelings
must simply be subdued or brought under. They must be
denied. They must be crushed. They must be squelched.
There is simply no place for them in the heart of the
Christian. In reacting thus, we make a serious mistake. For
one thing, Scripture gives us no warrant for doing so. Read,
for example, the prayers of the psalmists. The whole catalog
of emotions is freely expressed in those prayers. Anger,
resentment, discouragement, depression, unbelief, baffle-
ment, vengefulness, envy—they are all there—all, perhaps,
except lust. There is no attempt to cover them up, no
attempt to excuse them, seldom any effort to bring them
under control. In fact, the psalmists' prayers sometimes
seem so unspiritual to us that we could wish they weren't in
the Bible. But the prayers have one undeniable virtue: They
are honest. Perhaps if the psalmists had been better men,
their prayers would have sounded better in our ears. But
that's not the point. In prayer we must come to God just as
we are. There's not the slightest use doctoring up our
feelings so that they'll be presentable to God. Whom would
we deceive? God? There's nothing spiritual about bottling
up our feelings when we are alone with Him.

The experience of Jesus in the Garden of Gethsemane
(Luke 22:39–46; Mark 14:32–36) tells us the same story.
Even He, the perfect Man, does not try to change His
feelings to make them more spiritual. Without shame or
guilt, He pours out the anguish of His soul to the Father. His
heart quails as He faces the cross. His feelings rage and boil
within Him, even His sweat seems like great clots of blood.
He cannot crush those feelings. He doesn't even try. But in

the very midst of the battle, though He can do nothing with His feelings, He can still choose to do the will of the Father. And He does so choose. Are we to be more spiritual about our emotions than He?

In any case, squelching our feelings never pays. In fact, it's rather like plugging up a steam vent in a boiler. When the steam is stopped in one place, it will come out somewhere else. Either that or the whole business will blow up in your face. And bottled-up feelings are just the same. If you bite down on your anger, for example, it often comes out in another form that is much more difficult to deal with. It changes into sullenness, self-pity, depression, or snide, cutting remarks. Indeed, you often give vent to these things almost without realizing what you are doing and why: and then when someone reacts negatively, you are the picture of injured innocence. You haven't dealt with your anger yourself, yet you've made it impossible for the other person to cope with it.

Some even pride themselves on mastering their nasty, vicious tempers. But all they've done is to bury them deeper inside. When you do something that displeases them, they may refrain from flaring up at you, but you can tell that the old anger is still seething around inside. That anger, coupled with their self-righteousness, makes such people incredibly hard to live with. The old, straightforward anger or nastiness would have been much more tolerable.

Not only may bottled-up emotions come out sideways in various unpleasant forms, they also may build up pressure until they simply have to burst forth. When they do, someone is almost bound to get hurt. Some of us, for example, keep our anger or frustration in check for a while, determined to behave in a solid Christian way. But the longer we hold it in, the worse it gets. Then someone says or does some tiny little thing that constitutes the last straw, and we burst into a torrent of rage or weeping that's out of all proportion to the wrong done. We just couldn't hold it in a minute longer.

Some kinds of bottling up go even deeper than this, and have even more destructive results. I remember that for years and years as a Christian, I worked to bring my emotions under the Spirit's control. Over and over again, as they cropped up, I would master them in my attempt to achieve what looked like a gracious imperturbable, Christian spirit. Eventually, I had nearly everybody fooled, even in a measure my own wife. But it was all a fake. I had a nice-looking outward appearance, but inside, well, almost nothing was there, almost none of the life-giving power of the love and joy of the Lord. Way beneath, almost completely beyond the reach of my conscious mind, the mass of feelings lay bottled up. I didn't even know they were there myself, except when their pale ghosts surfaced now and then in various kinds of unsanctified attitudes and reactions. They *were* there nevertheless. And the time came when the whole works blew up in my face in an emotional breakdown.

Then all the things that had been buried so long came out in the open. Frankly, there was no healing, no recovery, no building a new life for me until all those feelings were sorted out and until I learned to know them for what they were. I had to accept them and find ways to express them honestly and nondestructively and under the lordship of Christ. No amount of prayer, yielding to the Spirit, or opening my heart to grace would do the job so long as I continued to deal improperly with my feelings. In fact, learning to walk in the Spirit, learning to live under grace meant precisely learning a new and more productive way of handling my feelings.

Let me repeat: The Christian way of dealing with feelings is neither to indulge them nor to crush them. To give in to our feelings is to hurt those whom God wants us to love. To crush our feelings sometimes hurts others more than we would have if we had vented them. But whether it hurts them or not, we are sure to hurt ourselves in ways God never intended us to be hurt. What then can we do with our feelings?

ACCEPTING FEELINGS

First of all, I must accept my feelings. They are part of the me that God accepts, just as I am. When God says,

"There is now no condemnation for those who are in Christ Jesus" (Rom. 8:1), He includes my feelings. Good or bad, beautiful or shabby, they're all included in the Atonement. That is, Jesus' death provides for forgiveness and healing of the disorders in my spirit that give birth to negative feelings. I don't have to hide them. I don't have to doll them up. They're just part of what I am, and God loves me as I am even though, as I say, He is at work to heal me, to change me into the image of the Lord (2 Cor. 3:18).

If we would stop and think about it, we would be amazed at the way throughout the Bible that God responds to genuine expressions of feelings. I can't think of a single place where God says or even implies to anyone, "Get hold of your feelings; I won't stand for that kind of emotion." One remarkable example of the opposite response occurs in the book of Job. Remember Job's sufferings, how he lost all his possessions and his children, and was afflicted with a loathsome disease. Then his friends came around and started criticizing him. The argument between Job and his friends runs throughout most of the book. Over and over in the anguish of his heart he cries out against God. His friends, on the other hand, continue to justify God's ways and tell Job that he is wrong. The interesting thing is that, at the end of the book, when God makes everything right, it is Job's friends whom God rebukes. "I am angry with you," God says, ". . . because you have not spoken as you ought about me, as my servant Job has done. So now . . . go to my servant Job . . . and he will intercede for you; I will surely show him favour by not being harsh with you because you have not spoken as you ought about me, as he has done" (42:7–8 NEB). The friends were busy spouting off all the right responses to God's ways, but from beginning to end they were way off base. They didn't understand what God was doing, and they were completely incapable of responding to Job where he hurt. Job in his misery was simply speaking the truth out of the deep pain within, and God saw past the seemingly rebellious words to the heart that was willing to trust even though God should slay him. God was not about to abandon or condemn Job simply because his feelings didn't match up to the ideal. God accepted Job just as he was because of his faith.

We must accept our feelings not only because they are a part of us—good or bad—that God accepts, but they should be accepted also as a part of what God created when He made us. God made us creatures of emotion, and He gave us our emotions for a purpose. He made us so that we would respond to injustice with anger, to danger with fear, to sexual stimuli with sexual desire. Every feeling we ever have is related to some need or hunger that God has written into our beings.

Now, it's true that because of sin we have distorted our feelings in all kinds of ways that God never intended. But even in their distorted, fallen state, our feelings are important. Even when they go sour—perhaps especially then—they tell us something that we need to know. They are, in fact, rather like pain on the physical level. They tell us when something is wrong. They tell us things we need to know about our psychological state. Their message is often very much harder to read than the messages our nerves give us. But we need to heed that message and make the necessary changes in our habits and our relationships. So we should thank God for our feelings. It's when we cease to feel that we need to start worrying.

This brings me to the next thing about feelings: That in and of themselves they are usually morally neutral. The fact that I appreciate a beautiful female figure or that I get angry when someone deliberately hits me in the face is not, spiritually speaking, an important issue. There may indeed be sin mixed in with my action. But I doubt whether the sin ever resides in the feeling as such. The sin, where there is sin, may be found either in the disobedience and negligence that produced the situation giving rise to the feeling or in our response to the feeling.

UNDERSTANDING THE CAUSES OF NEGATIVE FEELINGS

Our responsibility, then, as Christians, is not to fight our feelings but to learn to understand what produced them and then to learn to express them without transgressing God's law. If we focus our efforts primarily on our feelings because they seem to us unspiritual, then we are behaving like the person who tries to cope with pain merely by taking aspirin. Aspirin does help sometimes, but we'd be much better occupied finding the cause of the pain and putting a stop to it.

Besides accepting our feelings, then, we need to try to learn to understand what causes them. This may seem like a simple task. After all, we know very well what causes our negative feelings. We feel lust when our eyes or our thoughts turn toward sex. We feel anger when someone deliberately insults or injures us. We feel resentment when someone treats us meanly and we can't get back at them. We feel fear when we are threatened by a danger we cannot cope with. We feel frustrated when we are thwarted in something we desire to enjoy or accomplish.

But this does not give the whole picture. It does not tell us why sexual temptation sometimes is so overpowering, but sometimes not (often irrespective of one's level of sexual fulfillment or deprivation). It does not tell us why we sometimes fall into ungovernable rages over trivial matters, while at other times we can take serious hurts in our stride. It also doesn't tell us why some people fall prey to a resentment that eats up their lives, while others in similar circumstances seem to be able to rise above their resentments and learn to live happy, productive lives. What are some of the possible underlying causes of our emotional difficulties?

SQUELCHING FEELINGS

First, emotional problems may be, as much as anything, the product of squelching feelings. Learn to acknowledge those feelings and to express them non-destructively, and the whole picture begins to change. Feelings then become not enemies but friends, not masters but servants. But I won't belabor the point further. Just one warning. If you have been squashing your feelings all your life, you will find it an unbelievably demanding and protracted task to learn another way to act and react. Let me give you my own personal testimony that finding new responses to my feelings is abundantly worth the effort. It has made a world of difference in my relationship with God, with myself, with my wife, and with people in general.

FALSE SELF-DENIAL

A second important cause of emotional problems is false self-denial. This may sound as if I am flying directly in the face of the Lord's command to deny ourselves, take up His cross, and follow Him. And it may appear to run counter to the spirit of all those verses about turning the other cheek, going the second mile, seeking not your own, being meek and humble, and the like. Let me make it clear at the outset that I am in no way advocating disobedience to these commands. They are most emphatically descriptive of the kind of life God requires of us.

The problem is that there is a true and a false self-denial. The one springs from moral strength, the other from moral weakness. The one is an expression of genuine love, the other of cowardice and concern for one's "nice–guy" image. The person who practices the one has the power to stand up for himself but need not; the person who practices the other needs to stand up for himself but cannot.

The prime example of the moral strength that can deny itself genuinely and in true love turn the other cheek is Christ. See His kingly silence as He stands in the judgment hall accused of wrongs He never committed and soon to be nailed to a cross. No word of self-defense. No calling down fire upon His enemies. No fierce indignation. I used to picture Him in my mind's eye enduring all those taunts, suffering all that rejection, with tears in His eyes and His Adam's apple bobbing up and down over the misery and unfairness of it all. But I see Him so no longer. If there were tears in His eyes, it was for *their* miseries, not His own. For Himself, He was where the Father intended Him to be. He didn't *need* to feel sorry for Himself. He didn't *need* to answer back. He didn't *need* to stick up for Himself. He was too big for that. Not too proud, but too loving. This was meekness indeed. The real thing, all the way down to the depths of His being. And when the last blows fell, it was not "Father, how could they?" but "Father, forgive them." Surely here is how a king dies!

This is not the kind of self-denial that causes some of us to have trouble with feelings. I'm not talking about the genuine article, which Jesus possessed. I refer to our cheap, false substitutes. We think we are soaring in the heights of Christ's self-denial when we have not yet risen to the level where we can stand up for ourselves. Our self-denial comes not from genuine concern for the other person's welfare, but from our own impotence, and from a desire to seem sweet and Christian when we really are not. It's all a lie from beginning to end! Give me the robustly selfish person any day rather than the fake meek.

I have therefore come to take the position that those who are the fake meek are of all people the ones least likely to be able to obey the command of Christ to deny themselves. They have not yet found a self to deny. Before they can grow, they have to learn to fight. They will indeed have to learn true meekness eventually, but they are ill-occupied with the *meekness* lessons of grade 12 when they are not yet able to handle the *honesty* lessons of grade 1.

In short, false meekness is never the fruit of the Spirit. It always performs the work of the flesh. The real thing is something beyond price. It is always refreshing. Always healing. Always giving. May God grant us more of it.

OVEREXTENSION

A third case of emotions getting out of hand is overextension—committing oneself to more than one can handle, demanding more of oneself than one can reasonably be expected to perform. This overextension may itself rise from various causes. I may undertake more than I can manage because of what I call a *spiritual-giant complex*. For example, I hear of some saint of God who reads at least ten chapters of the Bible a day and spends at least an hour in prayer, carries a heavy schedule of employment, and spends much time in Christian work. So I commit myself to the same kind of schedule without ever stopping to think what my real spiritual stature and desires are. Or I may be driven by some perfectionistic ideal. I *have* to be efficient. I *have* to make every second count. Before I know it I find I've hardly allowed myself room to breathe. Or possibly my overcommitment comes from seemingly inescapable necessity or even from a genuine desire to please God. But whatever the cause I demand more of myself than my spiritual, emotional, and physical energy can handle. At such times what I need most is not victory over my feelings, but a change in my priorities and a change in my commitment level.

INSUFFICIENT RELAXATION

Another cause of destructive emotions, and one that often goes hand in hand with overextension, is insufficient rest, relaxation, exercise. Over and over again, for example, when I find myself feeling bored, frustrated, discouraged, out of sorts, I suddenly wake up to the fact that I have had my nose too close to the grindstone and have shorted myself on exercise. I take care of that need, usually by hiking if I can manage it, and immediately the whole world looks brighter. In short, regular relaxation and exercise is essential to mental and physical health. We pay the price when we allow ourselves to run short of this vital ingredient in our lives.

PERSONAL INSECURITY

Another cause of destructive emotions is our feeling of personal insecurity. If we feel inadequate, unacceptable, lacking in worth, there's no way we can maintain a healthy emotional life. Every criticism, well-meant or ill-intentioned, expressed or implied, tears us apart like a blunt knife probing an open wound. Everything that goes wrong throws us into a panic. Every neglect pierces us like a deliberate rejection. But I won't belabor the point. It must be obvious to the reader that God's grace is precisely the cure for this disease. In all the universe there's no better remedy.

SOUR RELATIONSHIPS

Destructive emotions can also come from sour relationships. Central to this matter is lack of grace. Where people don't accept each other, especially those who live or work closely together, emotional side effects are bound to come. If I reject or condemn someone else, try as I will, I can't keep from conveying this to him; and, unless the other person is unusually mature, he's going to respond in kind.

Here you have a ripe breeding ground for the whole range of nasty feelings. Somehow the grace relationship needs to be established so that love and respect can operate again.

DISOBEDIENCE TO GOD

An important cause of destructive emotions is disobedience to God, going against something that we know is right, resisting the prompting of the Holy Spirit. There's no way that we can persist in known sin and expect to come off unscathed. By all means we need to probe into the other causes of emotional problems that beset us, but while we are probing and before we have found any answers, we must flee the youthful lusts. We need to try to forgive that person who has misused us, to start that necessary but distasteful job we've been postponing, to take the step of faith or commitment to God that we know is the next stage in our Christian growth. It will do us no good to keep on nursing the anger of lust. It will do us no good to balk. We must persist in the attempt at obedience even if we fail over and over again. Grace is ours for the taking no matter how often we fail.

When we refuse the step of obedience altogether, we make a mockery of God's grace. How can we be enriched by a grace that we flout? In fact, if we refuse to obey, we need not be surprised if guilt plays all sorts of nasty tricks with our emotions and if hardness of heart eventually sets in and we lose our taste for the things of God altogether. Either way we have made enemies of the feelings God gave us.

Obedience, then, is a vital part of spiritual and emotional health. At the same time, however, let the reader beware of the common error of reducing almost all emotional problems to a simple matter of spirituality and walking in obedience to God. Many, many Christians seem to have the attitude that if a person is right with God he'll have no emotional problems. Conversely, if a Christian has problems, he is not right with God. He must get busy and set things right, we say. He needs to start believing God's promises, yield to the Holy Spirit, deal with known sin, establish a consistent devotional life, and so forth. Then everything will be all right.

Now, it's true that growth in true spirituality usually means growth in emotional health, but such growth seldom means that we can arrive at our goal simply by deciding we will subject ourselves to the lordship of Christ. We need not only obedience but understanding of the causes of our problems. We must know how to deal with the lack of self-acceptance and self-worth that contaminates every impulse toward spiritual and emotional health. We need the wisdom to perceive and deal with the habits of thinking, acting, and reacting that keep destroying us and our relationships.

Furthermore, an overready reduction of all things to the "spiritual" dimension can have unfortunate consequences. To judge everything on the gauge of spirituality opens the way to condemnation or rejection of those who have emotional problems. In effect, what we are saying to such a troubled person is that he shouldn't have such problems. If he'd get right with the Lord (like the rest of us?) he wouldn't have them. He'd get the victory over them. In such a manner we relegate him to the position of second-class citizen before God.

Also by our attitudes and actions we confirm in his mind a totally false concept of spirituality. Instead of exposing the sufferer to the healing power of God's grace, we tell him that his spirituality depends on his getting the victory in just those areas of his life where he is weakest. But we give him no help in reaching his goal. We throw Scripture verses and empty platitudes in his face, and then wonder why he can't seize them and find deliverance as we have. It's no wonder that many people suffering from emotional difficulties find God and Christian fellowship to be of little or no help. Worst of all is the irrelevant advice we give the person in trouble. We don't really understand his problem, but we're ready to hand out at the rate of a dime a dozen our pat answers and instant solutions.

COPING WITH NEGATIVE FEELINGS

I have suggested up to this point that feelings should be neither indulged by inordinate expression nor bottled up, but that we should accept our emotions and, so far as possible, understand them. But *how* can we cope with emotions?

Changing the subject

One way to cope with unmanageable feelings is to change the subject. Don't wrestle with them. Don't try to master them. Don't try to change them. Simply find something absorbing that you enjoy doing and give yourself to that for a while. Hobbies, for example, are often a godsend for beleaguered feelings. A person without hobbies is at a great disadvantage in facing the pressures and demands of life. One caution, however. Hobbies or other absorbing pastimes usually are therapeutic—provided they are not used as an escape to avoid facing problems that need to be dealt with. These are not likely to go away simply because we have found temporary relief through indulging in a favorite diversion. They may even get worse.

Expressing feelings nondestructively

Much more important as an antidote for the destructiveness of negative feelings is learning to express those feelings nondestructively. This is so beneficial that even such a seemingly ridiculous thing as a punching bag will help—or the time-honored expedient of going out to chop wood, or scrubbing the floors. If we do not express our negative feelings, they may go underground and take a terrible revenge on us. Yet if we express them freely without reference to their effect on others, we disobey the law of God and harm people in the process. What we need is a way of expressing feelings so that we neither hurt ourselves nor our fellows. How do we do this?

Accepting our feelings

The starting point, as I've already suggested earlier, is acceptance. If we reject our feelings as bad or unchristian, we will never allow ourselves the freedom to express them in any way whatsoever. By the same token, if we reject other people's feelings, we teach them that their feelings are wicked, and we force them either to conceal their feelings or carelessly to give vent to them when the pressure gets too great. Feelings are not to be rejected, but accepted, understood, even shared. Good, bad, nice, nasty—it makes no difference. Anything short of this breeds dishonesty or rebellion.

Telling God about our feelings

The next thing we can do is to tell someone how we feel, and the best place to start is with God. Here is Someone who we know understands every feeling we ever had and who still does not condemn us. So we need to learn to tell Him how we feel.

Most of us have, perhaps, been doing this ever since we first began to pray. But I wonder whether we have been going about it in the right way. We approach Him as if the feeling itself were somehow an insult to God or at least as if it were something that, primarily, we wanted Him to take away. In other words, we're not really going to God in order to express our feelings with someone who understands. Instead, we're basically going to Him for emotional aspirin tablets.

Worse yet, sometimes we try to pump up the proper pious feelings or attitudes as we take the matter to God. In other words, we try to change our feelings to suit Him. But feelings never turn on and off as a result of an act of the will. We cannot simply make our feelings change from one thing into another. Whom are we trying to kid anyway? Don't we think God can see through the silly hocus-pocus of manufacturing trust in Him when we really feel anxious? Or trying to create a forgiving spirit when resentment is burning deep down inside? No, we have to lay it right out on the table before Him, just as it is. Not that we need to fill *Him* in on the details as if He didn't already know the facts. It's *our* need. *We* need to express our feelings and to tell it just as it is. There must be no whitewashing, no euphemisms, no attempt to make the feelings look any better than they are.

This means that when I am discouraged, I need to go to God and say, "Lord, I'm fed up with my church responsibilities. No one ever responds when I try to get anything going. I feel like chucking the whole business. I'd like to crawl into a hole and pull it in after me." And when I'm angry with my wife, I need to tell God, " 'Lord, I'm so angry with her I can hardly see straight." Even when I'm upset with God, I need to go to Him and unburden myself: "Lord, I don't know why You let this happen to me. It isn't fair! You say You love me. Well, this doesn't look much like love to me. But, Lord, I want to believe in Your love. I just can't seem to see Your face anywhere."

If we learn to pray with this kind of honesty, we will find our whole concept of what He is like enlarged, and this will transform our relationship with Him. Also, we'll be amazed at how it serves to defuse the feelings. Chances are that the distress won't go away all at once, but a door will have opened so that God can work. We will have given Him a chance to let a little light into our minds and hearts so that we can begin to see things from a saner perspective.

Indeed, as we go to Him, we will find that He is more than a mere psychological safety valve; for He is a Father who cares for us, a Creator who understands us, and a Counselor who can help us. As we go to Him in anger, He helps us to see that our sense of injury need not touch the inner security and sense of worth that He gives. As we go to

Him with our fear, He shows us that "the angel of the LORD encamps around those who fear him" (Ps. 34:7). When we seek Him in despair, He gives us hope. Somehow He changes the whole inner landscape so that we can see things we never saw before, and seeing we find rest and heartsease.

But we do not always find deliverance in the sweet, effortless manner we might wish. God does not necessarily deal with our problems simply by removing them. Sometimes we have to take responsibility to do the things we know need to be done. Sometimes we have to struggle and probe until we understand the cause of our difficulty and then take appropriate action. But whatever it is that we need, God is willing to see that we get it, and His love and counsel will be ours in the process. We must therefore go to Him in trust and tell Him our problems, knowing that He is with us and that He cares and understands.

Telling people about our feelings

We need not only to tell God how we feel, we need to tell other people. Sometimes we may be tempted to think that, surely, it ought to be enough simply to tell the Lord. Well, it isn't. We can no more get along without other people in this area than in any of the others where we need their love and help. Conceivably, God's love could be enough for every need that we might have. But God didn't set things up that way. He gave us one another. Even Jesus, when He faced Gethsemane, needed His friends close by.

The trouble with talking only to God is that we so easily bring Him down to our level. If we're lazy and lax with ourselves, we imagine that God is indulgent, that He will give us a grandfatherly pat on the back. If we have a tendency toward self-hatred and self-condemnation, we see God as glaring at us when we come to Him. And, irrespective of our predispositions, many of us have been able to pray to Him for years without discovering the most fundamental facts about our attitudes, habits, and feelings— facts that become obvious to any halfway perceptive person to whom we open our hearts.

To put it another way, God puts His grace in the hands

of our brothers and sisters. He delegates to them the authority to pass on His kindness, His acceptance, His forgiveness. But, like it or not, understand it or not, it simply does make a difference to express your feelings to someone else. Almost anyone will tell you so. I remember counseling a Christian girl who was faced with very serious family problems that repeatedly got her down. She couldn't understand why she found so much relief from opening up to me but didn't find it from opening up to God. Yet that's the way God made us. We need to see His grace embodied in a person; we need human ears to listen to us and human lips to tell us about that grace before we can really understand it. That's part of the reason why Jesus had to become part of the human race, and our needs haven't changed since He came.

So far I've been talking about sharing our feelings with someone who can listen and understand—a third party who is not actually involved in the situation that gave rise to the feeling. But our need to express our feelings to another person does not end there. We also need to be able to express ourselves to those who hurt us or make us angry. I'm not, of course, suggesting that we ought to express *all* our negative feelings toward anyone and everyone who bothers us. This would be bound—at least sometimes—to lead to unfortunate and destructive results. But a close relationship is always destructive in a family or work situation where one or more of the parties cannot express feelings when wronged. It may sometimes be necessary to endure a situation like this, but, necessary or not, it is harmful. Out of it can grow all kinds of frustration, bitterness, resentment, loss of self-respect, self-hatred, backbiting, backstabbing, and the like.

In view of dangers of this kind, it behooves those in positions of authority or who are naturally more aggressive or self-assured to be considerate and helpful toward those who are not. This is especially important in the marriage relationship or between parent and child. It means learning to listen acceptingly and to encourage the other person freely to express the way he feels. When the other person does express unacceptable emotions, it means cutting out the condemnation, the tut-tutting, the sermons, the unsolicited advice, the comments as to how unreasonable the feelings are. What's called for is understanding, support, love, and a helping hand. Most of us have a great deal of growing to do before we can do this honestly and effectively.

But to return to the problem of our need to express our feelings: Sometimes the pressure of our emotional need is so great that we have to take the risk of sharing our feelings with someone. Then if the other person responds with acceptance, understanding, and respect, trust is born. But if not, trust dies. Next time we will keep our feelings to ourselves. We will prefer the danger of suppressing feelings to that of expressing them. But openness, honesty, fellowship, love will all be dead. And the imprisoned feelings will do their destructive work. We do well to remember that this is what we do to one another when we betray someone's confidence.

In short, I suspect that almost all of us would be healthier emotionally if we could learn to express our feelings more freely. We need to break through our fears. We need to destroy the delusion that we have of our own emotional self-sufficiency. We need to keep taking the risk. We don't have to open up to everyone, but we can try to find a person or group of people whom we trust. Where the cost of betrayal is not too great we can start learning to share little things. We can feel one another out, and in relationships where we find acceptance and mutual trust we can begin to go deeper. Be assured that when we begin to make the attempt the rewards are not long in coming. The risk, if taken with care, is abundantly worth taking.

Expressing one's feelings must also be undertaken with due respect for those to whom we tell them and for others not present who might be involved. For the sharer is not the only one whose hurt must be guarded against. I have, for example, sometimes told my wife of feelings and attitudes that were totally devastating to her, and it turned out that the feelings were only temporary. If I had really needed to share those feelings, I might better have done so first with my pastor or someone else who was totally trustworthy.

Sexual feelings and feelings that imply rejection of the other person are feelings that require special care and consideration in the sharing.

Finally, when we reveal our feelings to those who have hurt us, we should take special care to avoid using our anger or frustration as an occasion to put the other person down or to put him under a legalistic standard where he has to earn his way back into our good graces.

Two Basic Rules

Before I leave the subject of expressing feelings, I should like to suggest two very simple rules—rules that will help one to express negative emotions with honesty, but without using them as an occasion to lash out at the person who has hurt us or to put him down. The first is this: Never say, "*You* are bad," but say instead, "*I* hurt."

The second rule is this: Instead of saying, "*You* ought," say, "*I* want," or, "Would you please?" Now it may be true that the other person ought to do this or that, and if his love were perfect he would do what he ought without having to be asked. But to say, "You ought" is all too often to take the way of pride, and it can scarcely ever produce the desired response—at least not genuinely. There's no grace in it. On the other hand, to say, "I want," is to take the way of love and humility. It sets the other person free to express the love that he has, and this is what grace is always willing to do.

Not allowing feelings to dominate us

One last caution. When I make all these suggestions about what to do with feelings, I do not mean to imply that feelings should ever have the last word. We need to understand our feelings, accept them, and express them. We need to take them into consideration in planning our activities and commitments. But we do not need to let them dominate us. We need to recognize the fact that sometimes our feelings do not accord with the realities of the external world. (We get angry when no one has wronged us. We become fearful when there's really nothing to fear.) And sometimes they would lead us to harm our fellow human beings or shirk our duty or leave God out of account. At such times we need to acknowledge our feelings, not as enemies, but as facts. Nevertheless, we must obey God and follow the path that love dictates. After we've poured out our anguish before God, we must, like our Master, say, "Your will be done." It is better to enter into life with our feelings maimed at certain points, than to choose the path of destruction where eventually not only our feelings but everything else is lost. In the final analysis, if we really love God and people, we will follow the path of obedience and not be driven aimlessly hither and thither by changing feelings. If we understand our feelings and treat them accordingly, they can themselves become agents of health and energy in the service of God. They make very poor masters, but they make excellent servants. Let's use them intelligently, prayerfully, and in obedience to the One who gave them to us.

10 | *FAMILY RELATIONSHIPS*

No thoughtful reader can have read this far without recognizing the crucial importance of the home as a place for learning grace—or contrariwise as a breeding ground for non-grace. Here more than anywhere else the life of grace or of antigrace is demonstrated with almost irresistible power. Here the child learns the kind of acceptance that frees him to learn genuine love and responsibility, or here he learns the kind of rejection and condemnation that puts him on the defensive and makes him react with hostility, aggression, withdrawal, falsehood, slavish submission, and the like. Here, too, husband and wife enact the mutual respect that builds them up or the disrespect that tears them down. The mere physical proximity and the continual interdependences force the issues of love, acceptance, and respect in a manner that cannot be evaded. Superficial civilities will not do. The respectable mask will not answer. The realities and demands of living together necessarily obtrude into almost every facet of life. True attitudes and motivations are unmasked, and these inevitably have their healing or destroying effect upon every member of the family. It is essential, therefore, for all concerned, that grace become a living reality in the home.

CHRIST THE HEAD OF THE HOME

The first requirement for building a Christian home where grace reigns is to make Christ the head. There are homes, of course, where grace operates even though no relationship exists with the living Christ. But if we Christians are to know grace in its fullness in our family relationships, we cannot cut ourselves off from the source of grace, from Christ the fountainhead from whom all grace ultimately flows. Christ must be the head of the home.

This means not only that parents teach their children about God and about the grace He has revealed in Christ; but also that they live a life of fellowship with Christ in obedience to Him, learning to know Him as a person, and learning to live in the light of His grace. It means listening to the Holy Spirit as He speaks to them in their hearts and through Scripture. It means talking with Him in prayer. It means helping the children come to know Jesus and to establish a vital and growing relationship with Him. It means sharing as a family in fellowship with Him—a united fellowship that meets the needs of each member of the family at his or her own level. And it means expressing grace to one another in the day-by-day relationships in the home.

This last need, expressing grace in day-by-day relationships, is perhaps the most difficult task of all and the one for which least help seems to be available. I should like, therefore, to deal with the problem of how to express the grace life in relationships between husband and wife and between parent and child.

THE HUSBAND-WIFE RELATIONSHIP

In the husband-wife relationship as in all others, there's only one place to start:

Mutual acceptance

Husband and wife must accept one another just as they are, freely, totally, and unconditionally. With such acceptance, all other problems can be resolved. Without it, nothing else can. Yet condemnation and rejection come so easily, and they can be expressed in so many different ways: the quiet put-down, the cutting remark, the scathing rebuke, the nagging, the contradicting, the blame-pinning, the belittling, the cold politeness, the stony silence, the cataloging of wrongs, the steady pressure of oughtness and disapproval, the preaching and (God forgive us) the quoting of Scripture. The list could be added to and enlarged upon, but perhaps there is no need. We all know what it feels like to be subjected to such treatment. The point is that they all convey condemnation and rejection. They're all deadly. And if we're to experience grace in the marriage relationship, they all have to go. Without mutual acceptance, there can be no mutual growth in love and grace.

However, two kinds of non-grace behavior are particularly relevant to the marriage relationship. One is the *reformation urge* and the other is the *master-servant attitude*.

The reformation urge

Some people seem to have an almost irresistible urge to reform or improve their partners in some respect. The wife wants to make her husband more socially acceptable or to take more responsibility around the house. The husband wants his wife to be a better housekeeper or less of a gadabout. So the attempt at reformation begins. Sometimes even the tiniest habits seem to require corrective action: the way one dresses, the way one walks, the way one squeezes a tube of toothpaste. I'm not, of course, suggesting that we all don't need to change and grow in hundreds of different ways. The problem comes when the husband or wife appoints himself or herself a committee of one to see that the necessary change is enacted, and in doing so says, in effect, "You must change; I can't really accept you as you are until you get busy and do it." The result is that grace is smothered and all genuine desire for love-motivated change is undercut.

I must confess that this pattern was for many years an all too familiar one in the relationship between my wife and me. She was always after me to take more responsibility around the house and to plan things more effectively. I was always concerned about her volatile disposition—her tendency to blow up at what seemed to me the least little thing, and even to be angry at God for the things that He allowed into our lives. For years she nagged at me, and for years I preached at her. Behind the nagging and the preaching was the implacable "ought to" that each of us hung permanently over the other's head.

Let me tell you that none of this ever did either of us any good. Oh, we each made a few outward changes in conformity with the other's demands, but we never got to the heart of the matter. The problems were merely driven underground, and bitterness remained to sour and destroy our relationship. The time did come, however, when we finally learned, in a measure, to accept each other just as we were; but, oh, the sorrow to realize what we'd been doing to each other for so many years. How it warped us and robbed us of our joy in one another and in the Lord!

Now, since we accept one another in a new way, it has been amazing to see what the Holy Spirit has been able to do for us. For my part, I now find that I am much more ready and willing to take responsibility around the home than ever before, and I've seen my wife's whole attitude and outlook change. She is now finding life-giving meaning in the Scriptures with which I once unwittingly destroyed her.

No, it's not for us to take on the job of reformer in our relationship with one another. The Holy Spirit can do a much better job of it, and we need to learn to trust Him. Our part is to provide the background of acceptance that leaves the Spirit free to work. When God accepts us as we are, this acceptance frees us to become better than we are. Just so in our relationship with one another. By accepting one another, we free each other to grow.

This is not to say that we must always keep silence concerning one another's faults. We can talk about them, and sometimes we *must* do so. In fact, it's only mutual acceptance that makes it possible to do so productively. We, therefore, can and must express our feelings. We can even make deals with one another: "If you keep the kitchen floor clean for me, I'll keep the car washed"; "I'll fix the screen door this evening if you'll mend my socks." Such deals may sound terribly hard-nosed and even selfish, but they avoid the danger of oughtness pressure, and they provide a way of accepting one another's weaknesses and desires and of dealing with them as they really are.

The master-servant attitude

In some cases, grace is crowded out of the marriage relationship by the need that one of the partners seems to have to dominate or be served by the other. The husband, for example, may assume a sort of lord-of-the-manor role. The wife merely exists to take care of the husband's needs, to wait on him hand and foot. She is allowed no opinions of her own; they must agree with his. And if she has outside interests, they must be pursued in such a way that he is never inconvenienced. Even if it is necessary for the wife to work, she is still his servant. She comes home from a hard eight-hour day, and she still has to cook his meals, wash his clothes, darn his socks, and clean the house. But when he comes home from a day no more demanding than hers, he sinks into his easy chair with a sigh, puts his feet up, and waits for his wife to bring him his slippers. In due time he is fed and then he spends the evening in front of the television, working in his shop, or out with the boys. After all, doesn't the Bible say the husband is supposed to be the head of the house? So he goes his own way, luxuriating in his role, and wondering why his wife is so difficult to live with.

Let me say for the benefit of husbands who have tendencies in this direction that the scriptural view of the headship of a man over his wife is as different from the above as night is from day. His headship, and all headships for that matter, means *service*: not being waited on hand and foot but sacrificing oneself, not bossing one's wife around but giving one's life for her. It means doing for her what God does for every one of us: giving of himself to free the wife to grow and be what God created her to be (Eph. 5:25–33; compare also John 13:1–17). It means being precisely the opposite of the lordly male basking in self-satisfaction as the wife works her fingers to the bone for him. Even the Son of Man Himself came not to be served but to serve and to give His life as a ransom for many.

Sometimes it's the wife who seeks to dominate. Usually

she doesn't try to get her husband to do all the housework and cooking for her, but she does treat her husband as if he merely existed for her convenience. He's there to smooth out all the pains and frustrations of life. He's a buffer for her against reality or he's her tool to enable her to achieve her ambitions. In short, he's little more than an extra pair of hands and feet. He has no right to a will or opinions of his own unless they happen to coincide with hers. If they do not, she shames, nags, manipulates, or bullies him until he conforms. But whatever she does she is making an accepting, loving, motivating relationship impossible. There is no grace in it.

THE PARENT-CHILD RELATIONSHIP

It is almost impossible to talk about the grace way of life without seeing and talking about its relevance to rearing and caring for children in the home.

As I have suggested, a large part of the child's attitude toward life, toward himself, toward others, and even toward God comes to him as a result of the way his parents treat him. Furthermore, the child has to be taught almost everything by his parents from the ground up. His habits, attitudes, values, and behavior patterns often have to be deliberately shaped by them. He has to be brought to maturity by them. So the presence or absence of grace is bound to have a profound and permanent effect upon the kind of person he grows up to be.

In this shaping process, the question naturally arises: "How is a parent to convey grace to the child yet deal adequately with his selfishness?"

Let me say here that both the conveying of grace and the dealing with sin and selfishness are of vital importance. Neither one of these can be omitted without extremely serious harm to the child. Without the acceptance of grace, no values or standards can ever be truly transmitted to the heart of the child, for the parental demands then create an insecurity and hostility that can only undermine the parents' efforts. As long as the child feels rejected or condemned by his parents, he cannot produce for them the kind of love that must always lie at the heart of all true righteousness. "Do not exasperate your children," Paul tells us (Eph. 6:4), and we must heed his words.

But the fact remains that the child's selfishness must be dealt with. For, let's face it, a child can at times be obnoxious, self-centered, and even downright cruel. The parent renders him no service by treating him as if he's never anything but God's gift to the universe or by letting him get away with everything he may see fit to do or say. If the child never sees his selfishness for what it is, how can he learn the true meaning of the law of love? Even grace itself becomes meaningless. Such a child is not about to thank others for their undeserved acceptance of him, for he knows little about those faults in himself that might make acceptance a problem. He is convinced that all the good that comes to him is owed him or else it is won by his own strength and charm. Grace, therefore, is not so much the antithesis of dealing with a person's selfishness; rather it is the only possible ground for doing so. Sin must be dealt with, and grace is the only framework within which such dealings can be effective.

CONVEYING GRACE TO A CHILD

Let me make some suggestions for getting grace across to a child.

Accept the child as he is

First of all, the child must be accepted as he is. This means accepting him whether he's gifted or retarded, quick or slow, sensitive or thick-skinned, responsive or withdrawn, placid or tempestuous; when he's up, when he's down; when he's good, when he's bad; when he's happy, when he's sad. There's nothing that gives him a better chance to grow and achieve his full potential than a background of acceptance—total, unconditional, unchanging, secure. By accepting him as he is, the parent makes it possible for him to become better than he is.

Avoid condemnation and rejection

Acceptance of this sort means that parents must learn to avoid types of behavior that spell condemnation or rejection to the child: the worm technique, blame-pinning, oughtness pressure, nagging, preaching, and various types of rejection punishments. This avoidance of condemnation and rejection places a heavy burden of responsibility on the parent. It means, first of all, that the parent will have to change a great many automatic reactions. It's one thing to see that nagging or blowing up at the child is destructive; it's quite another to quit doing it. Even when one knows what to do, the old ways of reacting keep bursting out and destroying as they come. I can only say that it is worth the effort to keep trying. New habits do come in time, and God's loving presence is with us as we continually make the attempt.

But usually more than time and determination is needed. There also must be careful thought. New insights and techniques must be developed for dealing with hostile feelings and with irresponsibility or selfishness on the part of the child (to say nothing of the parent's own quota of the same). These new insights and techniques have to deal effectively with the problems that arise in living with a child and bringing him to maturity.

One thing, however, is of particular importance if the parent is to avoid conveying condemnation and rejection to the child. That is sensitivity to the child's reactions and feelings. This is essential because a child may take as condemnation and rejection something that is, in fact, not intended that way at all. Furthermore, what one child takes in his stride may utterly crush another. It is therefore impossible to lay down prescriptions for dealing with all children or all situations. The parent's dealings with the child have to be carried out with a deep understanding and sensitivity to the actual feelings and reactions of each child.

Accept the child's feelings, and help him to handle them

Another part of conveying acceptance and grace is the need to accept the child's feelings—especially his negative feelings—and help him learn to express them nondestructively. The child needs to know that his feelings are understood and that they matter to the parent. Above all, those feelings should not be squelched or preached at. But at the same time, the child needs to be taught that certain desires and wishes cannot be granted (sometimes because they are impossible, sometimes because the rights and wishes of others are involved), and that there are certain ways of expressing feelings that are damaging, both to himself and to others. He needs to know how to handle those feelings, how to express them without doing harm. This means, above all, giving the child a chance to talk about his anger, frustration, and fear with the assurance that he will be understood. It means taking time to find out what's bothering a child, patiently drawing it out of him, and helping him find release. This is a big order, especially when the parent's own feelings are so often involved, and the parent himself has not yet learned how to cope with his own feelings adequately. But if we are to express grace in the home, this is what we must begin to learn to do. We must look to God and then start trying to do what we know to do regardless of how hard it is and how long it takes us to learn.

Demonstrate love in action

If grace is to be demonstrated in the home, it will never be merely a passive thing. Acceptance by itself is not enough. In fact, it is meaningless to talk about accepting another person and then refuse to give oneself to meet that person's needs. God so loved that He gave, and it's only because He gave that we have any concept of His grace at all. Just so, the parent must give of himself to his child. Not just money. Not just toys. But time, concern, a listening ear, an open heart, and patient, unstinting help in the time of need. It means hours and hours of living, talking, working, playing together. It means sleepless nights, ceaseless prayer, patient discipline. It means giving, giving, and giving again—beyond desert, beyond expectation, and without hope of return. Grace must always express itself in self-giving love.

Give plenty of encouragement

Every child needs encouragement. There are so many ways in which he is inadequate, so many things he cannot do or understand. And there are so many forces in the world that put him down. True, he needs discipline sometimes. True, he needs to face the things in himself that need change and correction. But if there is too much discipline, too much punishment, he is unlikely to be able to learn the most worthwhile motivation for action—self-giving that comes from a loving heart. So when he does something well, he needs to be told about it. When he makes genuine progress, he needs to know it. He needs to know that his efforts are appreciated. Every child thrives on encouragement. Every child needs plenty of it.

DISCIPLINING A CHILD

To say that a child needs grace conveyed to him by his parents is not to say that he needs no correction, no discipline. When I plead for grace in the home, I am by no means advocating a blind, overly optimistic permissiveness. In fact, it's precisely because there are things about the child calling for discipline and change that grace is so essential. How then is the parent to discipline a child without, in effect, denying the reality and credibility of grace and without undercutting the power of grace to produce the desired change? Two things stand the parent in good stead here: the use of rules and the judicious use of cause and effect (that is, rewards and punishments).

The use of rules

Ordinarily, parents must clearly spell out rules or demands regarding the kind of behavior that is acceptable and unacceptable. It does no good simply to turn the child loose to follow his own pleasure. Nor is it reasonable to tell him merely to follow the law of love. He doesn't yet know what love means in all the situations he faces. He doesn't know what selfishness means. There's no way he can yet understand what it costs his parent when he scribbles all over the living room wall or when he smashes a prized antique vase. Nor does he understand the dangers with which his environment is fraught. To begin with, of course, his environment must be carefully restricted so that he cannot do serious harm to himself or to others. But, sooner or later, he has to be allowed a certain liberty. "You may scribble on the blackboard but not on the walls." "You may play in the backyard but not in the street." "If you want to go play at Jimmy's house up the block, you must ask Mother's permission first."

These rules, wisely suited to his ability and stage of development and lovingly but consistently enforced, are essential to the child's well-being. They are indeed restrictive, in one sense; but in another sense, they free him to grow, to learn, and to enjoy life without bumping into problems and difficulties he's not equipped to handle. They also allow the parent a clear-cut basis for dealing with the child strictly on the ground of rewards and punishments without having to overload him with expressions of anger, reproach, disapproval, disappointment, and the like. Finally, rules give the child a necessary security that comes from a clear understanding of what is expected of him, from the assurance of living in a reasonably predictable universe, and from the certainty that someone really cares about what he does and does not do.

So rules are a necessary part of a child's development. But it must be recognized that rules, though necessary, must be temporary. They should remain in force only until the time when the child can safely and wisely make his own decisions. Sooner or later he must learn to handle matches not as a no-no but as a necessary though dangerous tool for lighting fires. Eventually the prohibition against going out into the street must be canceled, and the child must learn to watch out for traffic. The teenager must learn to go to bed at a decent hour, not because his parents tell him to, but because he wants to be alert and fresh for the demands of another day. And he must call home at night to inform his parents of his whereabouts, not because he is required to do so, but because he knows they care about him and because he cares about them. It has to be left up to him. He either does these things of himself or not at all. Rules cannot be left in force forever.

In view of the importance of rules, and their temporary nature, I find it instructive that God Himself, in choosing out a people for Himself, saw fit in the time of their infancy to govern them with rules: "Thou shalt. . . ." "Thou shalt not. . . ." But the time came when He freed them from those rules. Now we are no longer under the law, but have come into our inheritance as mature sons and daughters (Gal. 3:23–4:5; 4:13–25).

Creative use of cause and effect

Rules in and of themselves are not enough to enable the parent to ensure the kind of behavior that he wishes from the child. There must also be enforcement, and the tool for enforcement is creative use, by the parent, of cause and effect. In other words, the parent sees to it that certain actions on the part of the child have certain effects brought about by the parent. The parent determines that certain kinds of behavior will have certain consequences, and then manipulates those consequences so that the child will learn what he needs to know. For example, if he goes out into the street when he's not supposed to, he gets paddled for it. If he misuses crayons, he is not permitted to play with them for a certain period of time. If he goes to Nancy's house without permission, he is forbidden to go out next time. If he breaks the neighbor's window, he has to pay for at least part of the cost.

This is all obvious. Parents have been doing this kind of thing since time immemorial. The point is not *whether* the parent makes use of cause and effect in these ways, but *how* he does it and whether he is able to manipulate the consequences in such a way that the child really learns from the experience without any serious loss of the love relationship. This requires considerable sensitivity and creativity. The following are a few suggestions for using cause and effect more effectively.

Avoid rejection or condemnation punishments

Sometimes parents attempt to modify their children's behavior by various kinds of punishments or scoldings that intentionally or unintentionally spell rejection or condemnation to the child. Such punishments may indeed be successful in getting the child to stop some kinds of undesirable behavior, but the price is to nullify grace. That is too high a price, and we have already seen some of the dreadful consequences this can have.

Punishments of this kind may include things such as refusing to speak to the child, giving him a merciless tongue-lashing, and the like. It also includes all brutal or excessive punishments. For example, a child leaves his coat lying around in the living room, and his parent clouts on the side of the head or soundly thrashes him. Any punishment that comes through as excessive or unfair carries with it over-tones of rejection—an unwillingness on the part of the parent to take the trouble to understand the situation and realize what things look like from the child's perspective.

Furthermore, certain punishments spell rejection to some children but not to others. Even such a simple punishment as spanking may have a variety of meanings to different children. For some, spanking may be a salutary experience that leads to significant changes in behavior and carries with it no special overtones of rejection. To others it may simply be one of the vicissitudes of life that one learns to take in stride. It scarcely constitutes a punishment at all. To still others, especially children who are particularly sensitive and anxious to please, it may be so harrowing and soul-searing that they are almost unable to undergo it without a sense of rejection. In other words, if a parent is to avoid rejection or condemnation punishments, he must be sensitive to the effect that any given punishment has upon his child.

Make the punishment fit the wrongdoing

If punishment is to be effective, it must be appropriate to the wrongdoing. By this I do not mean that the child should necessarily suffer exactly according to the suffering he has caused (an eye for an eye), though there may be cases where something like this is appropriate. I mean, rather, that the punishment should correspond to the wrongdoing in such a way that the child is enabled to see the real meaning of what he has done. Thus, if the breaking of a window calls for punishment, it would be much better to make the child pay (if he can) for at least part of the cost than to bawl him out or spank him or confine him to the house for the afternoon.

Suit the punishment to the child

Any punishment should be suited not only to the deed but also to the child—to what he can understand and to what proves effective in his particular case. Spanking or any other punishment will not be equally effective with everyone. What works with one child will not work with another. And vice versa.

Especially important, of course, is the age of the child. To the younger child, for example, a verbal rebuke or spanking may be about the only thing that works. There's no way he can be made to understand the significance of the things he does wrong. All he knows is that his parents don't like what he has done; he doesn't know why. He doesn't understand that when he scribbles on the living room wall it means hours of time and effort that his mother or father can ill afford. All he knows is that he has done something bad. At that stage, that's all he needs to know. Later he will need to know more. The point is that the punishment should be geared to what he can understand and appreciate at his particular stage of development.

Suiting the punishment to what the child understands and to what proves effective for him is, of course, a demanding task. It requires an enormous amount of thought and understanding on the part of the parent and a great deal of willingness to experiment. The parent has to keep trying one thing after another until he finds something that works. He may also need to do extensive reading on child training or consult with other parents to learn what they have done in various situations. I confess at this point that I am doing the easy thing by sitting in my chair spouting off general principles. The really hard part comes when the parent gets down to the business of trying to make it work. My hat goes off to those who are really working at it.

Handle emotions wisely

The handling of emotions in the disciplining process is by no means a simple matter. On the one hand, emotions have to be expressed. The parent must be honest with his feelings, and the child needs to know, at times, how deeply the parent feels about some of the child's misdeeds. On the other hand, emotions can easily be expressed harmfully or be used in ways that are damaging to the child.

Some parents make it a rule never to discipline the child in anger. This is fine if discipline in anger necessarily means overreacting and treating the child unfairly. But often it means that the child never learns to appreciate how deeply the parent feels about some of the things he does, and it may turn out that the parent never really deals adequately with the misbehavior. The occasion is past and there no longer seems to be any point in doing much—except, perhaps, to deliver an ineffectual or (what is equally undesirable) a guilt-inducing sermon.

Problems come when feelings are used either to put the child down or as a sort of weapon to force compliance. In the former case, the parent reverts to rejection and condemnation. In the latter, he exercises a sort of moral tyranny or oughtness pressure to make the child conform. It is much better simply to deliver the expected punishment and be done with it. It's better to leave off the heavily charged, condemning emotions and let the child face the consequences that the parent brings to bear upon him. It's precisely the impersonality and the inevitability of the punishment that enables the child to retain his self-respect and to avoid feeling that he has forfeited his parent's love and acceptance by his misdeed.

Accentuate the positive

I have been focusing primarily upon the judicious use of punishment as one of the ways to influence behavior. However, the parent should never come across as one whose chief function is to discipline wrong behavior. Life for the child should include plenty of warmth, plenty of love and affection, plenty of appreciation. There is also room for concrete rewards for demonstrations of good behavior. I have a friend, for example, whose daughter could not for a long time be cured of a persistent habit of clinging to her mother all day long, no matter what she was doing. Reprimands or punishments accomplished nothing. The parents finally solved the problem by giving the child a penny every time she succeeded in holding herself in restraint for a stipulated period of time. The child soon found she enjoyed the challenge, and before long her behavior changed to the point where clinging was no longer a problem.

The danger of this type of treatment is that the child may get so that he behaves properly merely for the sake of reward, not because he cares about what he is doing. Particular care, then, must be taken to insure that the child does not acquire a permanent habit of needing external reward for activities that should be inherently rewarding in and of themselves (such as Bible-reading, pursuit of knowledge, musical expression). I, for my part, shall always regret the fact that grades came to occupy such a large part in my motivation for doing schoolwork. Much of the joy of reading and learning were inhibited for me by this undue emphasis.

Make the child increasingly responsible

In the long run, the parent is not aiming at implicit, unquestioning obedience, necessary though this may be. He is aiming rather at developing responsibility in the child. He wants the child to do the right thing because he understands it, believes in it, and cares about it.

This goal means, among other things, consciously

moving from the use of what I call "substitute consequences" toward those that are more and more real. By
substitute consequences I mean those that the parent
artificially produces as a response to a child's undesirable or
wrong behavior. For example, the real consequence of
running out in the street without looking is to get hit by a
car and suffer serious injury or even death. The substitute or
artificial consequence is the swat on the bottom or the
scolding that the parent administers. The real consequence of
the teenager's staying up all night is that the next day he is so
miserable and groggy that he's unable to do justice to his
schoolwork or other responsibilities. The substitute consequence is to deny him the privilege of going out the
following weekend.

Substitute consequences are a necessity during the time
that the child is learning how to live, and it's the parent's
duty to be creative in providing just the consequences that
are most appropriate and most effective. But these consequences can be only temporary. The parent cannot always be
spanking the child for wrongdoing. Eventually the child
must refrain from the wrongdoing, not in order to avoid the
spanking but because of the harsh demands of the real world.
So the parent must continue to aim more and more at the
real consequences and to lead the child to face them rather
than the substitutes.

The parent's job, then, is to provide consequences for
wrongdoing that approach more and more closely the reality
of the external world, and to let the child face those
consequences as he becomes able to handle them.

Set the child free

If the child is going to learn responsibility, he eventually
has to be set free to make his own decisions in the light of
real consequences, not merely in terms of parental displea-
sure or in terms of the rewards and punishments the parent
provides. For every child there is an optimum time for him
to be granted each type of freedom. If freedom is denied
beyond that time, either the child will be stunted in his
personal growth or he'll rebel. There comes a time, for

example, when he must be given freedom to choose what he will wear; a later time when he must choose his own bedtime hours; a time, too, when he should have use of the family car without supervision; and a time when he is free to marry whom he chooses. The general rule for the parent is to do his best to give the child the maximum freedom of which he is capable as soon as he can handle it.

Understand the long-range purpose of discipline

In all the struggles of disciplining the child, the parent must keep his eye on the ultimate purpose: to write God's law upon the heart of the child. The parent is not merely trying to produce a compliant, obedient child. He's not primarily trying to get the child to stop doing certain things that are bad and start doing certain other things that are good. Rather, he is trying to bring into full maturity a heart that understands good, loves it, and chooses it. He's not trying to win subscription to certain rules and standards of behavior; he's trying to win willing heart allegiance to the values that stand behind those rules and give validity to those standards. He's not trying to produce someone who will always meekly do what he ought; he's trying to create a free spirit that willingly chooses what he ought because he is committed, body, soul, mind, and spirit, to the love behind the ought.

If the parent is going to do this, he is, of course, going to have to demonstrate such love, such values, in his own life. No amount of rules and regulations, no amount of creative manipulation of cause and effect or of reward and punishment will be sufficient. There must be a demonstration of love in action.

Finally, the parent must determine to free the child to be what God created him to be. In the final analysis, the parent is not trying to corral something wild or to shape something nebulous. He is trying to free something beautiful to be just what God intended. May God give to all parents the grace to work diligently toward this goal.

11 | *BUILDING ONE ANOTHER UP IN THE CHURCH*

If grace is an urgent necessity in the home, so it is also in the church. For grace is not something that we can afford to limit to the safe, reinforcing confines of the home. Grace must break across family boundaries and touch others in an ever-widening circle of transformed, transforming lives. It needs to be the identifying mark of bodies of believers everywhere.

After all, how does a person, child or adult, learn grace? How did you yourself come to know the grace of God? My guess is that there were two major factors. First, someone told you about it (no doubt pointing you to the Scripture and to the grace revealed in Christ); then someone demonstrated it. Most of us have to have both. In fact, it usually happens that if you have the telling without the demonstration, the telling is nothing more than talk. Worse yet, if a person tells you one thing but demonstrates the opposite, he gives the lie to everything he says.

God knew that we need both the telling and the demonstration. For this reason He gave us not only the written message but also the Word made flesh. God had a message He wanted to convey so He told us about it through the prophets. But that was not enough; He had to send His Son. We had to see His message embodied in flesh and blood—someone we could hear and see and touch—Jesus the living Word of God. John tells us that when folk saw Him, they saw His glory, "such glory as befits the Father's only Son, full of grace and truth" (John 1:14 NEB). The grace of God had to be demonstrated, or people simply would never see it.

The same thing is true today. However, Jesus is no longer around on earth to give us that demonstration. He passed the job on to someone else—to the Holy Spirit who lives out the grace of God through us, His church. The church, therefore, is the place where God continues that demonstration. Not just individual believers, but the church, the visible, interacting, fellowshiping, serving, loving-one-another church—the church that is His body, the hands and feet of the living Christ. If the church falls down on the job, needy men and women, believers and unbelievers must live without that demonstration of the meaning and the power of the grace of God.

In this chapter, then, I'd like to focus my attention on the church, not as an obstacle to the grace of God (which, sadly, it often is) but as a living vehicle of it. This means that I will be talking about my concept of an ideal church and not about any church that any of us has ever seen. There was something very like such a church in the early days of Christianity, as described for us in the book of Acts. Others have approached the ideal with varying degrees of completeness. Yet even where the church falls short, we must remember that we have no right to condemn. Rather, our failings constitute a call to reach higher, a call to strive toward the ideal that Christ sets before us.

CHARACTERISTICS OF THE GRACIOUS CHURCH

What then would a truly gracious church look like? What would be the characteristics of a church that really demonstrates the grace of God? I suggest that it would have at least the following characteristics: Its people would be accepted and accepting; it would be open and honest; it would be giving and serving; and it would be exercising the gifts of the Spirit. This would not, of course, be the whole picture. But if these characteristics were in evidence, much more would follow. Let's look at each of them.

ACCEPTED AND ACCEPTING

The gracious church is one where its people know what it is to be accepted: accepted by God—a God who does not condemn them, but accepts them as they are. It is also one where people accept one another because God has accepted them without condemnation and just as they are.

I wonder whether we have any idea how radically important this matter of acceptance is. Is it not our hunger for acceptance that drives some of us to put on a "nice-guy" front? We strive desperately to act like the kind, obliging person at every moment. We say yes to a hundred commitments we don't really care about. We work at receiving favor from others. But all of this is little more than an attempt to hide from them and from ourselves our own sense of inadequacy or our fear of condemnation and rejection. Some of us are driven to join the rat race of keeping up with the Joneses. After all, what would people think of us if we didn't prove ourselves at least as capable and responsible as everyone else? Still others of us crush down our own desires and feelings for the sake of other people's good opinion. We scarcely even dare stand up for ourselves or express our convictions on important issues. Sometimes we hardly know what we do feel because we've squelched our feelings for so long.

Others of us follow a different tack altogether. For fear of rejection we climb into our little shells and shut the world out. We avoid responsibility because if we stuck our necks out, we might make a mess of things, and we'd never be able to look anyone in the eye again. We even avoid reaching out to our neighbors or those in need. "Maybe they don't want me sticking my nose into their business," we say. So we dare not take the risk.

Then look at the various ways we behave when we think that some have rejected or condemned us (how easily we imagine it). How sharply we react! Some of us come up with a string of excuses a mile long to justify ourselves. We may have sense enough not to spout off these excuses to any but our nearest and dearest; but there they are, seething and boiling in our minds. Or perhaps we specialize in the sarcastic put-down. You condemn me so I condemn you: the old eye for an eye and a tooth for a tooth. Or maybe we cut off the relationship, contenting ourselves with cold politeness on the occasions when circumstances force us to meet those who have hurt us.

Surely it is the acceptance problem that makes us go to such absurd lengths to hide from our own inadequacies. So often we can see everyone's faults but our own. Sometimes we try to tell ourselves that all is well and we don't care what people think, but we insist on this so loudly to ourselves that we give ourselves away. Some of us have to prove that we are bigger, stronger, or more capable than others. We can handle our problems. We can cope. We're not like those poor saps who have to curry favor with everyone. (But why do we have to work so hard to prove it?) Others of us try to give the lie to our inadequacy by bullying or pushing other people around. Still others who are either too weak or too proud to do this accomplish the same purpose by gossip. Somehow, it seems, if we can only prick the other person's bubble or expose his façade, we can prove to ourselves that we are better than he is, and perhaps not so bad as we had feared or as someone else might think. Then some of us boost our egos by setting other people straight. Oh, we all play our little games, but behind them is the acceptance problem—the unhealed wound of our empty hearts.

But this is a problem that grace solves. This is the very wound that grace heals. God has told us that when we put our faith in Him, He accepts us just as we are. There's no longer anything to excuse, nothing to run away from, nothing to prove. I don't have to convince myself, God, or anyone else that I'm better than Mr. Jones or not so bad as Mrs. Smith. The Creator of the universe Himself has told me that I am not condemned and never will be. "If God be for us, who can be against us?" (Rom. 8:31 KJV). This is the message of grace, the Good News of the Christian message:

God Himself has accepted me, once and for all; and my weary, anxious heart has rest.

Now because of this, because I *am* accepted, I am freed to accept my brothers and sisters. As long as I had my own acceptance problem, I couldn't really accept them. They were all the time upsetting me and rubbing the old wound raw. I couldn't feel their pain because of my own. But once that wound is healed, I can begin to think about them. I don't have to dwell on their inadequacies in order to avoid thinking about my own. I don't have to condemn them. I don't have to set them right. I can accept them as they are. Because God's grace has touched me, I can become the channel of God's grace to them; I can become part of God's demonstration to them of the meaning of grace.

Not only *can* I accept them, I will, I must. Not only the logic of grace, but the dynamic power of it forces this response. This is why Jesus tells us to forgive others, not just seven times but seventy times seven (Matt. 18:22). To be forgiven means to forgive. To be accepted means to accept.

Remember the story Jesus told about the man who owed his master millions of dollars, an enormous sum (Matt. 18:24–35). When the man couldn't pay, the master ordered him to be sold into slavery along with his wife and family. Everything he had was to be sacrificed to pay that debt. Then the man did what you and I would have done. He begged for time, and promised, "Lord, I'll pay every last penny if you'll only give me time." So the master, out of pity, and because he was gracious, freely forgave him and canceled the whole debt. He gave the man much more than he asked for. In a moment's time, the whole staggering burden was gone. But soon after that the man met a fellow servant who owed him only a few dollars—much less than one-tenth of one percent of the debt for which he had obtained the master's forgiveness. And he forced his fellow servant on pain of imprisonment to pay up. The man begged for time. "Just a little bit of time, and I'll pay you everything," he said. But no. Prison it was until the last penny was paid. No extension of time. No mercy. Immediate, ruthless justice.

We are naturally outraged at such behavior, and we are not surprised when the master rescinds his earlier forgiveness and sends the man to jail until the debt is paid. But the story beautifully illustrates the point: Forgive as you are forgiven. When the man refused to forgive his fellow servant, he indicated to the whole world that his master's forgiveness meant nothing to him. It hadn't touched his heart. It hadn't reached him where he lived. Just so, if we cannot forgive our brothers and sisters, we demonstrate that God's forgiveness has not yet reached to the bottom of our hearts. It has not yet touched us where we live. To experience forgiveness and grace is to pass it on.

OPEN AND HONEST

The grace-filled church is not only accepted and accepting, it is open and honest. Acceptance and honesty go hand in hand. Nobody wants to expose himself, his weaknesses, failures, needs, hopes, and fears to someone who does not accept him. But when you are with someone who accepts you wholly and unconditionally, just as you are, it immediately becomes infinitely easier to open up. It is natural. It is safe.

After all, why *do* we wear the mask? Why do we hide our real face, our real feelings from one another? Why must we pretend to be something that we are not? Why is there so little openness, so little genuine, heart honesty with one another? Is it not precisely because we fear that we will not be accepted or that we may prove ourselves unacceptable? As long as there is no grace, no acceptance around, you don't need to think I'm going to open up about the deep weaknesses, needs, and pains in *my* life. To do so would be folly. It wouldn't be safe.

I often wonder what it would be like if I were to dare to stand up in a prayer meeting and pray what I sometimes have really felt: "Lord, I've just had a terrible row with my wife. I didn't really want to come here to pray, but I felt that I ought to. And I don't really want to pray now. But Lord, You know how I feel. This is what I am, and if I don't come to You this way, I can't come at all. Please make something of this mess if You can. I can't."

Imagine what would happen if someone would pray like that! "Who'd have thought it? And I thought that Joe Cooke was such a spiritual Christian!" Or perhaps: "Uh-huh. I knew it! I knew that guy Joe Cooke wasn't all he was cracked up to be." Or possibly a well-meaning Christian would tell me afterward that he was praying God would give me the victory. How many would respond with real humility and grace, and thank the Lord for a breath of honesty and open their hearts to me—as if to say: "Welcome, Brother Joe. Join the club. Nobody here but sinners, and we're all drinking at the fountain of grace"?

Too little grace. Too little acceptance. That's the problem. And the result is that there is too little honesty and openness.

But when genuine grace is in the fellowship—genuine, unconditional acceptance—then openness and honesty become gloriously possible. You don't have to wear the mask. You don't have to pretend. You don't have to project the perfect Christian image. You can simply be what you are. Because your brothers and sisters accept you as you are, you can trust them. You can share your fears, doubts, and frustrations; and you will find love and encouragement. You know that they will accept you as you are. They are God's demonstration to you of what His unfailing grace means.

In short, where grace is, where acceptance is, there is honesty. Where honesty is, grace is free to work, to show itself for what it is. It isn't mere plaster images of sainthood that are being accepted. It's the real person—the struggling, failing, hurting, hoping person as he really is.

What I've been suggesting, then, is that grace makes it possible to share with one another, especially in the areas where we are weak, for our weaknesses are the point at which honesty and openness become a problem. They are the point at which honesty hurts. But where grace is, we can speak of our weaknesses.

We not only can but we need to do so. For one thing, it is urgent that we destroy the plaster-image notion of

Christianity—the notion that the good Christian is one who is always walking closely with the Lord, always happy, always victorious, never has any problems, never fails, never struggles like the rest of us; he's so spiritual, in fact, that he has passed beyond the need of grace. Frankly, if that's what a Christian is, that lets me out of the running right now. And I'm sure it shuts out a lot of other people, too. We may think that a few stalwarts will be left who really have the goods. But we think so only because we haven't gotten close enough to them. We haven't probed deeply enough.

The point is this: The Scripture tells us to confess our sins to one another (James 5:16). And we need to do it. Otherwise, we get a wholly false notion of what Christianity is all about. Some people, for example, get the absurd idea that they are the only ones who have difficulty living the Christian life or that if they could only be like the spiritual, faithful few, everything would be all right. Some even feel that they don't belong in the church at all because they are sure they can't make it like other people can. If we had a little more honesty in the church, we could squelch this lie once and for all. Jesus came not to call the righteous, but sinners (Matt. 9:13).

And let me say this: The leaders of the church should start the ball rolling. They are the ones who know best, from long experience, that they have not yet achieved perfection, that there are still many struggles, many failures, much pain. Having grown strong in the Lord, they have less need to fear the threat and pain of rejection and criticism. They should be the first to take the risk of owning up to their weaknesses and of confessing their faults to one another.

Another reason we should begin sharing our weaknesses with one another is the fact that only so can we discover by outward demonstration what grace means. As long as we keep hiding our true selves from our fellow Christians, just so long do we ward off all possibility of discovering from one another the meaning of grace. No one ever learns the joy and release of acceptance as he is when that person never lets anyone else know what he really is.

We leave no chink in our armor where grace can enter. We dare not put ourselves in such a vulnerable position as to be honest with one another and therefore dependent on grace. It cannot break through into our lives and heal our relationships with one another.

One word of caution: When I recommend confessing to one another, I am not suggesting that we should plunge in and indiscriminately confess everything under the sun. Confession, like sharing of feelings, should be conditioned not only by our own need and our trust in those to whom we open up, but also by the capacity of listeners to handle what we say. When we confess, we need to ask ourselves whether our action is likely to transmit grace and truth, either to ourselves or to others. Above all, confession should not be an effort somehow to earn the acceptance of God or people. To do so would be to bring in legalism under the guise of spirituality—and with deadly results.

One further comment on the matter of openness and honesty: Grace and acceptance not only make it possible for us to expose our own faults and problems, they also make it possible to be honest with someone else about his. One might think that grace, with its no condemnation, would tend to gloss over wrongdoing. You're not supposed to permit even a breath of criticism of anyone. You have to see everyone through a purple haze of sweet love and acceptance. *Not so!* Repeatedly Jesus rebuked His disciples for various things, especially for their spiritual obtuseness and lack of faith. He even tells us that if our brother sins against us, we are to "go and show him his fault" (Matt. 18:15).

Actually, only under grace is there any point in rebuking fellow Christians and telling them their faults. After all, if you go to someone you have condemned or rejected as a person, and tell him what's wrong with him, you most likely will get a string of excuses as long as your arm. But under grace, criticism can be constructive, and rebuke can bear good fruit. If someone rebukes me in love, without rejecting me and without putting me down, I can take it. I shall never forget a very dear friend who once read me the riot act about a lack in my Christian life. She was a very godly woman, and I knew she really cared about me. I knew there was no trace of rejection in her attitude toward me. So I took her rebuke like a lamb. I greatly profited from it. But only one in a thousand could have gotten away with it. It had been done in grace, and I knew it. Grace makes possible even this kind of openness and honesty. Nothing else will.

GIVING AND SERVING

The fellowship that knows the acceptance of grace will also be a giving and serving fellowship. This is one of the natural results of grace. Because you have been accepted, you can begin to forget about your own gnawing hunger for love. The gaping maw in the very center of your own heart has been filled. There's no longer a bottomless pit of need. Once your appetite for acceptance was insatiable. (The person with a serious acceptance problem always hungers for affirmation.) But now the problem of your own worth has been settled once and for all. Now you can begin to look at the world around you. You can begin to see other people's needs, and you have the heart to want to try to meet those needs. Besides, as a member of the fellowship, you are beginning to know what your brothers' and sisters' needs are. After all, grace has made it possible for them to tell you. They haven't kept their needs bottled up in their own hearts. They have been open and honest with you. So the person who has been touched by grace begins to give. He begins to serve. Grace has freed him to do this.

In fact, one could say that giving and serving are a part of the very definition of grace. It's the nature of grace to do this. "You know the grace of our Lord Jesus Christ," Paul says, "that though he was rich, yet for your sakes he became poor, so that you through his poverty might become rich" (2 Cor. 8:9). Again, we read that Jesus "did not come to be served, but to serve, and to give his life as a ransom for many" (Mark 10:45). Grace doesn't just accept; it also gives and serves. It's not merely a negative thing that says, "I

don't condemn you." It's not merely a passive thing—a great benevolent smile of acceptance. *It acts. It serves. It gives.*
    That's what God's grace meant when He gave His Son. That's what the grace of our Lord meant as He went about spending His time, energy, and finally His life's blood for us, who never deserved anything better than God's frown. That's grace. And to receive that grace is to pass it on. "Freely ye have received, freely give" (Matt. 10:8 KJV).

EXERCISING THE GIFTS OF THE SPIRIT

    In the church where grace reigns will be found not only acceptance, openness, and a giving spirit; there will also be a manifestation of the gifts of the Spirit. By the gifts of the Spirit I mean, of course, the various gifts that are given to different members of the body for the upbuilding of the whole. Paul mentions, for example, gifts of apostleship, teaching, prophesying, exhorting, administering, healing, tongues, and so forth. Gifts such as these should be in evidence in any church where the Spirit of grace has produced a community of accepted, open, and giving believers.
    I say these gifts *should* be in evidence. Perhaps I should say they *will* be. A gracious fellowship is one in which the members will indeed be exercising spiritual gifts, for grace leads to gifts. In fact, in several important ways these gifts are dynamically related to grace. If grace is really present and functioning, the gifts will appear and will be exercised for the upbuilding of the church; and the result will be more grace. If grace is not in the fellowship, the gifts will have no opportunity to grow. Or if they do appear, they will usually be abused and will fail in their purpose of ministering grace. Through the rest of this chapter, I should like to show in some detail the relationship between gifts and grace.

GIFTS GIVEN THROUGH GOD'S GRACE

    First of all, gifts are God's expression of grace to the church. Even the Greek word used in the original text of the

New Testament brings out this fact. The word is *charisma*.
You will recognize the word as one which has come into
English to mean a particular quality that certain people
possess, causing others to fall under the spell of their charm.
We used to talk, for example, about the charisma of
President Reagan. From the same root we derive the word
"charismatic" as in the expression *Charismatic Movement*,
referring to a movement in the Christian church that
emphasizes gifts such as those of healing and tongues. But
the word in the New Testament is used to refer to the whole
range of gifts—any gift that is given to someone for the
upbuilding of the body of Christ.

The interesting thing about *charisma* is that it comes
from the Greek word *charis*, which is the word for grace.
That is, the word *charisma*, as used in the New Testament,
refers to something that springs from grace. It is a grace
thing, something unearned, a free gift, a gift of grace. These
gifts, then, are things that spring from the grace of God.
They are unearned kindnesses that God showers upon us
because He loves us and wills to act graciously toward us.

What is there about these gifts, then, that makes it
appropriate to call them "gifts of grace"? In what sense is
God expressing His grace to the church when He bestows
these upon it? For one thing, as I have already pointed out,
grace means giving. God in His grace does a great deal more
than merely accept the undeserving; He keeps on showering
kindnesses upon them; He keeps on giving to them of His
bounty. It is the nature of grace to do so.

These gifts to the church meet such a deep need. And
they accomplish so much. Each of us needs help in the
process of growing in grace, and these gifts provide that
help: here a word of encouragement, there a helping hand;
here a listening ear, there an act of hospitality; here a word of
rebuke, there a word of exhortation; here an inspiring
challenge, there solid biblical teaching. All of these are
provided by a host of different people, all of whom have
learned to love me and to serve me, each in his own special
way.

Furthermore, these gifts meet not only individual needs,

but the needs of the whole body. We aren't a group of individualists, each doing his own thing off by himself. We are a body and it's only because we function as a body that the various needs are met. No one person can meet all my needs. Not even my wife. Certainly not the pastor; he's much too busy meeting a crowd of other people's needs. Different people meet different needs. As Paul says, "The eye cannot say to the hand, 'I don't need you!' And the head cannot say to the feet, 'I don't need you!'" (1 Cor. 12:21). On the contrary, every member contributes something and every member is needed. We are a body. And the body has hundreds of needs, which no one member, be he ever so gifted, can ever hope to meet. So we each contribute something to the body, and the whole body grows. As you share your gift with me, not only do I grow, but so do you; and so do all those who are praying for me, and watching the Lord work in me; and so do all those who are praying for you and watching the Lord work in you. As Paul says again, "Bonded and knit together by every constituent joint, the whole frame grows through the due activity of each part, and builds itself up in love" (Eph. 4:16 NEB). Truly, when God gave to the church the gift of grace, it was a rich gift— one that went far beyond what any of us could have deserved.

But the gifts more than meet our needs, both individually and corporately; they also confer an almost incredible honor upon us. They are God's way of carrying on *His* work. We become members of the body *of Christ*. He doesn't merely save us, and then squirrel us away somewhere where we'll never get dirty or where we'll never get into trouble again. Rather, He leaves it up to us to carry out His purposes in the world. As Jesus once took on a human body to reveal God's love to us, so now He indwells His body—the church—to continue through us the work He began. We are His hands, His feet, His eyes, His mouth, each one of us functioning as distinct organs, each constituting an indispensable part of the body, and all together doing the will of the Head. This is what the grace of God has done for us in pouring out His gifts upon the church.

GIFTS AWAKENED THROUGH GRACE

The dynamic relationship between grace and the gifts of the Spirit may be seen not only in the fact that God, in grace, gives these gifts to the church, but also because grace, by its very nature, awakens them. When grace awakens the human heart to new life, it inevitably awakens the person's gifts, too. Similarly, when grace begins to function vitally in a community of believers, it will awaken gifts in that community. Let us discuss first how this works in the heart of the individual; then I'll take up the problem of how this works in the body.

GIFTS AS THEY AFFECT THE INDIVIDUAL

Consider, for example, what happened to Paul when he first met the grace of God. Prior to the Damascus Road experience, he was obviously already a very gifted man. There can be no doubt that he had a keen mind and a ready tongue. He must already have begun to display some of the powers of reasoned argument that were later to become so characteristic of his preaching and writing. In fact, surely almost all of the gifts he later exercised as evangelist, pastor, teacher, and apostle were in evidence. But these were not gifts of the Spirit. They were not gifts of grace. He did not *know* the Holy Spirit. He had not *met* the grace of God. The Paul who was later to use these gifts to build up the body of Christ had not yet been born. He was still a mass of contradictory passions, all warring together in his soul. Those gifts, those natural abilities—great though they were—could be used only for the destruction of the body of believers.

But what happened when grace met him? All those warring passions became unified. Those tremendous gifts were freed to be what they were created to be. They could serve the body of Christ and build it up. Almost immediately he began to exercise the gifts of an evangelist, proclaiming Jesus publicly in the synagogues (Acts 9:20). "More and more forceful," he grew, and "silenced the Jews of Damascus with his cogent proofs that Jesus was the Messiah" (Acts 9:22, NEB).

However, I suspect that Paul was not yet ready at the time of his conversion to exercise the gifts of teaching and apostleship. He had yet to spend his years in Arabia and elsewhere, probing deeper and deeper into the meaning of grace. Then when grace had more fully penetrated his mind and mastered his heart, he was ready to become the apostle of grace to the Gentiles. But in both cases, whether at his first encounter with God's grace or at the later one, grace freed the natural gifts Paul had; grace awakened them, and grace put them to the service of the body.

That's what grace does to all our natural gifts. It awakens them and transforms them. Instead of destructive forces, they become constructive. Instead of expressing our neuroses or feeding our ambition, they become a demonstration of God's love to and through us. We become alive and useful because God's grace has touched us and changed both our reason for doing things and the way we do them.

The whole process could, with a couple of provisos, be summarized by the formula:

NATURAL POTENTIAL + GRACE = GIFT OF GRACE

The provisos are, first, that the Holy Spirit is the effective agent in transforming natural potential into gifts of grace. He is the one who makes real to us the meaning of God's grace, and thereby awakens into spiritual life the potential that God first created in us. It is He under whose lordship these gifts must be developed and exercised. The gifts are not only called gifts of grace, they are also called gifts *of the Spirit*. They are all the work of "one and the same Spirit, who apportions to each one individually as he wills" (1 Cor. 12:11 RSV).

The second proviso is this: that certain gifts seem to fall outside of the equation I have proposed. I am referring to the special, miraculous gifts, such as the gift of healing, the gift of speaking in an unfamiliar language (as occurred on the day of Pentecost), the gift of predicting the future. (I use the term "predicting the future" rather than "prophecy" because the gift of prophecy, according to scriptural use, refers more to preaching or proclamation. It would also include proclaiming God's Word in a more general sense, in the manner that the Old Testament prophets did.) These are, of course, gifts of the Spirit, too, and they clearly are given as a gracious gift of God to the church. However, it would be difficult to maintain that these are natural gifts awakened by the transforming power of grace. They seem rather to be special endowments conferred in grace, by the sovereign will of God, without any very obvious reference to natural endowments.

I find it useful, therefore, to distinguish two types of gifts: the special-endowment gifts (miracles, healing) and natural-endowment gifts (preaching, teaching, administration). I repeat, however, that when I use the term "natural endowment," I do not mean that the person untouched by grace and unled by the Holy Spirit can produce them as a gift of the Spirit. As I said before, these gifts do come from natural endowments, but only when those endowments are awakened and transformed by grace and exercised under the lordship of the Holy Spirit for the building up of the body.

So far as I can tell, the list of natural-endowment gifts is open-ended. That is to say, there is no final, complete listing of all of them. Certainly Paul, in the three passages where he deals with gifts, makes no attempt to provide a complete list. Each of the three listings (1 Cor. 12–14; Eph. 4; Rom. 12) is different from the other two, and it is plain that Paul was merely pulling examples from the hat, as it were.

In comparing the two types of gifts, my personal opinion is that the natural-endowment gifts are the everyday bread-and-butter gifts in any given fellowship. The special endowment gifts are different. They seem to be given by God to particular persons, to particular fellowships, or to the church at large for special reasons that may be obvious only to God. It does seem, however, that at major turning points in God's program for His people, these special, miraculous gifts seem to cluster. The miracles of the Old Testament (though we might not want to call them "gifts of the Spirit") clustered around the times of Moses and Elijah, both of which were great crisis times for Israel. In the New Testament they clustered around the time of Christ and the apostles when God was doing a completely new thing in the world. Even nowadays one hears reports of special manifestations in particular areas of the world where apostolic outpourings seem to be taking place.

I am saying, therefore, that there seem to be times of cosmic importance when these special gifts are particularly in evidence. But to say this is *not* to say that God cannot give such gifts at any time to particular persons or fellowships of His choosing. After all, the Spirit distributes gifts separately "to each one, just as he determines" (1 Cor. 12:11).

He is the one who chooses. So although I have never been present in any group when such gifts were exercised, I am willing to believe that God is still working in this way today, and I would rejoice to see more of such evidence of God's presence among us in power and grace.

Yet, as I have suggested, the natural-endowment gifts are the bread-and-butter gifts. They should be a part of the everyday life of every church. Every member has such potential gifts, and every member should be experiencing the grace that awakens this potential, transforms it, and makes it available to the rest of the body.

Now back to my formula:

NATURAL POTENTIAL + GRACE = GIFT OF GRACE

Let me illustrate my point by showing how it works in the case of two or three of the gifts.

Take, for example, the gift of teaching. Here we have a gift that clearly draws heavily, though by no means exclusively, on natural human potential. A person who exercises the gift of teaching in the church is almost sure to have certain, preexisting natural gifts that are pressed into the service of the Lord. Such natural gifts might, for example, include a keen mind, the ability to express oneself effectively in speech, and the ability to draw out other people's ideas and facilitate discussion. A person may perhaps be a good teacher without one or another of these abilities. But if he lacks them all? I must say that I doubt it. It's true that sometimes a person's abilities may lie latent and undiscovered until the Holy Spirit puts them to use. It's true also that these abilities can be sharpened by training and practice, and that their lack can be partially compensated for by effort, sincerity, and self-giving love. But the fact remains that, normally, the Spirit makes use of natural abilities that He chose for us before the foundation of the world, and wrote into our beings when we were first conceived. These natural endowments are the raw material He has to work with in creating gifts for us and for the church.

But until the Holy Spirit sets these natural endowments on fire by the grace of God, they cannot be called gifts of the Spirit or gifts of grace. What happens, then, when grace touches the combination of natural abilities that make a person a potentially good teacher?

First of all, grace gives a new content and perspective to the teaching. The teacher has discovered in grace a glorious, life-changing truth about God and His ways, and every part of his understanding has been affected by it. He has something glorious to say, and he longs for a chance to say it and teach it. It's true, of course, that one can teach the Bible without having experienced God's grace. In some ways one can even teach it rather well—history, geography, cultural background, literary characteristics, intellectual content, and the like. But if the teacher hasn't understood and experienced God's grace, he is lacking the one vital ingredient that is necessary before he can truly build up others in their faith. He simply cannot do this kind of building up because he has no faith of his own to share. On all the vital issues of God's ways with individuals, with the church, and with the world, he will miss the crucial point. He will have plenty of facts to contribute, plenty of knowledge, plenty of understanding of one kind and another, but no life. If believers are built up under his teaching, it will be only, as it were, by accident or because of the vitality and understanding that they already possess. They will not have received it from him.

Second, the understanding and experience of grace puts

new motivation into one's teaching. The teacher has met the
God of grace, and he wants to serve Him. He has met and
understood His grace, and he wants to share it. He has
accepted God's children as his brothers and sisters, and he
wants to serve them. He no longer wants or needs to boost
his own ego by showing his vast knowledge or by putting
down those who have less understanding than he. Everything that he is and has is at the service of the body to
communicate not only facts, not only knowledge, but life—
the kind of life that can come only as a result of knowing and
growing in the grace of God.

Let's look at another gift—hospitality. Now, this is
something that is actually urged upon all of us. The writer to
the Hebrews tells us, for example, "Do not neglect to show
hospitality" (13:2 RSV). That is to say, we should all work at
it; we should all be as hospitable as we can. At the same
time, it is clear that some of us have special gifts along this
line. Some people naturally love to cook, to plan ahead, to
open their homes to guests. They seem to have a knack for
anticipating others' needs and making them feel at home. We
all know people like this.

Without grace, these abilities can degenerate into a kind
of self-service. A person may exercise hospitality merely to
make a big impression or to keep up that reputation as the
best cook around, to display generosity or to pay back a
social debt. Without grace, hospitality is never a genuine
giving to one's fellows. And without the God of grace, it
never becomes a sharing of God's love for human beings in
need.

But when God's grace is central, hospitality becomes a
sharing of the unconditional love of Jesus. When I speak of
sharing Jesus' love, I don't mean that one communicates no
love of one's own—as if one were to offer a cup of cold
water in Jesus' name, caring nothing for the other's thirst but
doing it only because Jesus expects it. I mean that because
God's love has touched us, we are enabled to have some of
that same kind of love. If this is so, there will be no
ostentation in hospitality, no putting on airs, no one-upman-
ship, no restricting our hospitality to those to whom we owe

it or to those who can repay us in kind. It becomes a free and glorious giving to those in need, sharing the love of Christ through our own genuine, unfeigned, unconditional love. Grace has taken the natural gifts that go together to make up hospitality and has transformed them for the service of the body.

GIFT OF TONGUES

Perhaps it will be helpful to look at one more gift, the gift of tongues. Not the kind of tongues in which one miraculously speaks in an actual foreign language unfamiliar to the speaker, but the kind where one speaks an unintelligible "heavenly" language. I am a little reluctant to broach this subject, not only because so much has already been written on the subject but also because I myself have never spoken in tongues. I do not have the credentials of Paul, who could say, "I thank God that I speak in tongues more than all of you" (1 Cor. 14:18), and then could go on to correct various abuses of this particular gift. Nevertheless, I should like to try to shed additional light from a grace perspective. In doing so, I shall assume that the tongues experience may, under certain conditions, be a valid expression of God's grace to the believer.

In order to help us see the tongues experience in a new perspective (new at least for some of us), I suggest that speaking in tongues is one of the natural capacities that people have; and, like other such capacities, it can then be transformed into a gift of grace by the Holy Spirit. The experience, *in and of itself*, is not necessarily either divine or diabolical, any more than the practice of teaching, exhorting, administering, offering a helping hand, or even taking a bath for that matter. It is simply human. Under certain conditions people are susceptible to it or capable of it. It is found in many parts of the world, both as a Christian experience and as a non-Christian experience.

What, then, makes speaking in tongues a spiritual gift? Two things. First, it is a spiritual gift when it springs into action as the result of a genuine encounter with God or a

genuine experience of grace. Speaking in tongues then
becomes a heart response to the grace of God, an experience—sometimes ecstatic—of prayer and worship of God.
(See, for example, 1 Cor. 14:14.) Second, it is a spiritual gift
when it ministers grace not only to oneself but also to
someone else. Hence Paul's demand that the gift of tongues
be exercised in public meetings of the body only when
someone is there to interpret (vv. 1–19).

GIFTS AS THEY FUNCTION IN THE BODY

Up to this point, I have been talking about the way in
which grace awakens gifts in the individual. It also awakens
gifts in the body as a whole. That is, when grace is really
functioning in the body, that grace will give birth to a host
of gifts by the very dynamic of what grace is.

As we have already seen, grace leads to giving. Because
our deepest heart need has been met by God's unconditional
acceptance, we have been enabled to see one another's needs
and have begun to give ourselves to meet those needs. Not
only so, but the openness and honesty in the fellowship has
enabled us to know in a much deeper way than would
otherwise be possible just what those needs are. Also,
because God has given so freely to us, we are given the heart
and the desire to give freely to one another. Then as we start
giving, what do we find? We each discover in ourselves and
in one another those unique gifts that God gave to each of
us. We give what we have to meet a need that we see, and it
turns out that each one of us has his own special thing to
give and his own unique way of giving it. Some have facile
tongues. Some have quick minds. Some have ready hands.
Some have understanding hearts. Whatever it is that we
have, somewhere in the body is some person—or group of
people—who can benefit by it. It doesn't matter what the
gift is, it is bound to be used. Even the seeming ugly
ducklings among us turn out to have something special to
contribute. No two persons are alike, and no one is left out.
There is no one in God's family who holds his place there in
vain. No culls and no repeats. And it's because we are a

gracious community, occupied in giving to one another, that we discover those unique capabilities in ourselves and in one another.

God isn't in the mass-production business. He doesn't turn us out like cars off an assembly line or coins from a mint—a hundred million dimes all identical—same size, same shape, same weight, same date, same inscription, same face, same materials—all indistinguishable from each other. Never, never, *never*. (We are told that even with the billions of snowflakes He creates, no two are alike. How much more is this true of His sons and daughters!) All of us are different, all loved, all valuable, all useful. And so we are bound to differ in gifts, for God has created us with different gifts. If it were not so, we could not be a body. We'd just be one big eye gazing balefully at the world or one big mouth spouting a single monotonous message.

So we were created unique, each one of us; and this uniqueness blooms within the gracious community. It was always there in potential, but until the gracious community called it into service, it was a small wizened thing or perhaps a twisted, warped, even vicious growth (like Paul's gifts before he met the Savior). Then as we begin to give ourselves for one another, we discover one another's uniqueness. For my unique gift comes to me, not only as a gift from God, but as a gift from you. I give myself to you, and I find I don't lose myself in the process. Instead, I grow. I would never have known I had the gift of teaching unless I had tried to share with you the insights God has given me, and had seen your eyes light up and your life change as a result of what I gave. You would never have developed a grace-informed gift of hospitality if you hadn't begun to reach out to me and many others to give of your love by welcoming me into your home. You have helped me find out who I am, and I have helped you find out who you are. If we'd each been busy doing our own thing without reference to one another's needs, we would never have found ourselves. We have proved in our experience the truth of the Master's words, "Whoever wants to save his life will lose it, but whoever loses his life for me . . . will save it"

(Mark 8:35). It is thus that grace in the body awakens the unique gifts in all of us.

GIFTS AN EXPRESSION OF GRACE

Another way in which grace is linked with the spiritual gifts is the fact that the gifts are themselves expressions of grace. They are ways in which we share the grace of God with one another. They are ways in which we serve one another without reference to what is deserved or owed. We do it not from obligation, but because we love one another; and love *gives*. The gifts, then, are our love gifts to one another. As I said before, if any of us is going to learn what the grace of God means in our daily lives—if that grace is to become a vital, living thing—we need to experience it. We need to have it demonstrated. We need to see it not only in Scripture or in the life of Christ, but also embodied in people we meet in everyday life. We need to experience it not only in our private devotional lives, but in our lives with one another. The gifts are where we get that experience. They are the living, personal vehicles of God's grace to each of us.

This is why, wherever in Scripture we see the gifts discussed, we always find an emphasis upon love. When Paul teaches about gifts in 1 Corinthians 12–14, we find him over and again stressing the need to exercise gifts in such a way as to build one another up (see especially chapter 14). And it is no accident that, right in the middle of his teaching on gifts, he breaks off into his unforgettable description of love in chapter 13. This chapter *had* to come right there because that's what gifts are all about. If we use the gifts for any purpose other than building one another up in love, we are prostituting them.

The same emphasis occurs in the Ephesians passage on gifts. At the conclusion of the passage Paul says, "Bonded and knit together by every constituent joint, the whole frame grows through the due activity of each part, and builds itself up in love" (4:16 NEB). And the same thing appears again in the Romans 12 passage. The first words Paul says after discussing the gifts are: "Love in all sincerity"

(v. 9 NEB). In short, love simply cannot be separated from the gifts. That's what gives them their meaning.

And that love, if it is to be genuine, must be gracious. It must give of itself freely without reference to what is earned or what is deserved. Love, because it is love, must express itself in grace to all whom it touches; and the gifts are the vehicles that love uses to convey that grace.

12 | *BUILDING A MEANINGFUL FELLOWSHIP*

Alas! To describe a grace-filled church, as I have done, is to realize how far short of that ideal most of our churches fall. Some churches are beginning to experience this kind of life and fellowship, but most of us have scarcely ever seen anything like this in action. What can be done to build more grace into the church? And what can we, as individuals, do when we find ourselves in a church where very little grace is at work? These are the questions I should like to touch on in this chapter. To answer them fully would require at least a whole book, but I shall confine myself to a few suggestions that I hope will be of help.

REQUIREMENTS FOR BUILDING A FELLOWSHIP OF GRACE

The first question I wish to touch on is this: What does it take to build grace into the church? How can a given church be changed from a mere preaching post, or a sort of Christian club, into a genuine fellowship of grace? I shall simply mention a few requirements for such change, and then deal more fully with the major problems.

One requirement for building a genuine fellowship of grace is the *committed leadership and example* of a few people in the fellowship who have been truly touched by God's grace—people who have had a genuine encounter with Christ, who have come to acknowledge Him as Lord, whose lives have been changed by grace, and who through the Spirit are learning what it means to walk by the grace standard, both in their relationship with God and with others. No group can become a grace-filled body of believers without such a nucleus of Christians at its core.

Another requirement is a *vision*, shared by the leadership of the church and by many of its members, as to what a grace-filled fellowship can be. We must clearly understand what the Scriptures teach about the church, experience a deep hunger to realize the scriptural ideal, and be willing to pray and labor sacrificially toward that goal. Before a church can have that shared vision or be hungry enough to work toward it, people must be *taught*—months and months of solid teaching on the nature of grace, the nature of the church, and the nature of gifts.

But teaching is not enough. They must see a *demonstration* of how it all works and be exposed to the kind of acceptance and self-giving love that will make them want more of it. This kind of thing is not learned from preaching. It is caught by infection. The few people in a church who have been most deeply touched by grace and have caught the vision of what real fellowship might mean must pass it on, not only by word of mouth but by love in action.

Finally, the *church needs to be structured,* or perhaps restructured, to facilitate the new kind of life. I do not propose to go into any kind of detail as to what this restructuring might mean. Others have already done this job far better than I can. (There are many fine books on church renewal including *Full Circle* by David Mains; *Brethren, Hang Loose* by Robert C. Girard; and *A New Face for the Church* by Lawrence O. Richards.) I will, however, mention one thing: The restructuring will have to involve a greatly increased emphasis on small groups, e.g., home Bible-study groups, support groups, age groups, interest groups, fellowship groups, missionary circles, prayer groups, work groups, service groups, and the like. It does not much matter what the groups are, provided they are small (ideally six to twenty people) and that they are composed of at least a nucleus of people who are committed to the lordship of Christ and to caring for one another. They must be consciously seeking to learn the meaning of acceptance, honesty, giving, and developing and using their spiritual gifts. I know that many people are suspicious of small groups, and I am the first to admit that they have their problems and dangers. But I do not know how the kind of grace life I have been talking about can grow solely in the midst of a large mass of Christians, however committed, and however spiritual. It can grow only where individuals really know and care about one another; this cannot take place en masse. I see no workable alternative but to go for small groups. I know from experience how richly such a group can contribute to one's Christian life and to the life of the church. There is nothing like it.

The above, then, are some of the things that are needed if a church is going to develop the kind of grace life I have been talking about. I hope the brevity of my remarks has not led you to think that I am giving pat answers or glib diagnoses. Behind what I have said is a whole world of the gracious and painstaking work of the Holy Spirit, and a world of discussion, study, prayer, thought, planning, struggle, and sacrifice on the part of those through whom the Spirit is working. Let no one think that the desired change is going to be either quick or easy. But the goal is abundantly worth reaching for, and God's blessing and power await those who humbly and prayerfully move toward that goal.

OBSTACLES TO THE FELLOWSHIP OF GRACE

Before we can move toward that goal, however, we must deal with three important problems or misconceptions. These are *individualism, organizationitis, and pastoritis.*

Individualism

The first problem is individualism: the good old American spirit of self-sufficiency, the spirit that says, *"I can and ought to handle all my own problems."* It reflects the ideal of the self-made person—competent, self-assured, beholden to no one. Our whole life pushes us in this direction. Each person has to make his own living, take care of his own house and yard, provide his own transportation, and solve his own problems. If he needs help, he should pay for it. There's even something right about this. Society could never survive if no one took responsibility for his own needs, and nothing is more contemptible than the person who can provide for himself, yet sits back and sponges continually off of other people.

Nevertheless, it is a fact that none of us is entirely self-sufficient. It wasn't our own doing that we were born with healthy minds and bodies, and none of us could have reached adulthood without the help and the love of others stronger and more able than we. Even as adults we all have emotional and spiritual needs that can be met only by the love, kindness, and acceptance of others. We cannot purchase these, yet if we don't get them, we are the losers. We suffer an impoverishment for which no amount of power and competence can compensate; we simply cannot understand—much less live—the grace life on our own. *We need one another.* We need the kind of acceptance, honesty, and mutual giving and receiving that only an interdependent body of believers can provide. We're members of the same body. The hand cannot do without the eye nor the eye without the mouth. We are dependent upon one another. We are not self-sufficient.

One deadly effect of the individualistic, self-sufficient ideal is the almost impossible strains it sometimes places upon the marriage relationship. All the needs that could be met by a host of different people, each contributing something different, wind up having to be met by one's spouse. The spouse has to be friend, helper, confidant, counselor, errand-runner, and a host of other things. He or she has to meet a conglomeration of needs that neither one can bear. It's no wonder that many marriages break under the pressures they are subjected to.

In the long run, the ideal of individualism or self-sufficiency is self-defeating. After all, what happens when everyone is self-sufficient and looks out strictly for himself?

Inevitably a few strong, exceptionally capable people get ahead. They win the power, the prestige, the wealth, the influence. But what happens to the rest of us? A few of us fight fruitless battles against entrenched power and influence. A few resort to backstabbing. A few of us withdraw and live our own cozy little lives. But most of us wind up conforming. It's the only thing we can do. If we want our own small share of the good things of life, we have to conform to those who are wiser and more powerful. Sometimes we make a few gestures toward independence; sometimes we pretend that we are self-sufficient. But in the main we conform. We keep on doing what is expected of us, presenting the proper image to the world around us. As a nation, we treasure the ideal of self-sufficiency; but actually we have become a nation of conformists. We cling to our precious individualities, but in doing so we've been forced to sell ourselves out.

How different is the life of a fellowship of grace! Here we are giving ourselves to one another, each esteeming the other better than himself, no one clinging to his own individuality, but each looking toward the good of the other. Yet each in so doing becomes the unique self, the total person that God created him to be. It's the old story once more. He who saves his life loses it, but he who loses his life finds it. If we are to embark on life in a fellowship of grace, we must surrender our self-sufficiency and give up our cherished individuality. Only in so doing will we ever find the far greater sufficiency, the greater individuality, that God gives.

In fact, the grace life is utterly impossible so long as we cling to our self-sufficiency, for this spirit is almost the exact antithesis of grace. The self-sufficient person *earns* the right to acceptance by his own ability and competence, not through the generosity of another. Having earned his acceptance, he is almost certain to insist on accepting another person on the same basis—and then only if the other person's ability and power in no way threatens him or shows up his own deficiencies. As for any deficiencies he himself may have, the last thing he is going to do is to let someone else see them. He will preserve the self-sufficient image at all costs. True honesty is for him a total impossibility. And when it comes to giving . . . well, why should he give? If other people want something, let them work for it as he did! Even if giving does take place, it becomes either a strict trade—value given for value received—or a way to express superiority and power. It's not the real thing, *because there's no love in it.*

Perhaps the greatest disaster takes place when the ideal of individualism and self-sufficiency creeps into the spiritual life. Everyone is supposed to be strictly responsible for his own spiritual welfare. If a person isn't making it, there's only one answer: "Get with it! Get right with the Lord!" No one is supposed to have problems that he and the Lord can't handle between the two of them. "On the Jericho road," as the song goes, "there's room for just two./No more and no less; just Jesus and you." But it's a lie! There *is* room for more than two. There are others on the road, and all of us need one another as we travel along. God never meant us to go it alone. That's what the church is for. We fall into this snare of spiritual self-sufficiency and individualism only to our deep peril and impoverishment. We need each other, and we need to live accordingly.

Organizationitis

The second problem that undermines the accepting, giving, gift-oriented life in the church is what I call *organizationitis.* This is a disease in which the main effort and concern of the church and its members are devoted merely to keeping the organization going. An enormous amount of time, money, thought, and effort is expended in all kinds of efforts directed almost entirely toward this one end. We have endless projects and committee meetings. We plan things and rope any number of people into any number of offices. We call meetings. We launch expensive building programs. But a good deal of it seems not to be going anywhere and few seem to respond.

Then all too often our only solution to this lack of response is more effort, more organization, more plans.

Fewer and fewer people are putting out more and more effort but with fewer and fewer results. Then the next step is our condemning ourselves for failure or condemning others because of their unwillingness to pitch in and help. Why isn't something happening? Why don't they respond? Why won't others take responsibility?

We seem to think that by effort and organization we can produce life, whereas actually these only express life. If life exists, it will grow. It will be infectious. It will produce other life. And then an organization can be built to accommodate that life so that it can grow and express itself more effectively. But organization does not create life. It cannot express a life that isn't there.

The problem is not that anything is wrong with organization as such. The difficulty arises when organization assumes center stage, when it begins to become an end in itself. In the final analysis, organizations are intended to serve the needs of people—not the other way around. So people must be our first concern. How can we express the love of Christ to them? How can we serve them? How can we help them grow?

If our primary concern is people, then we must try to meet their felt needs. It does no good to render services in which they have no interest or to provide activities for which they have no appetite or to ask their help with activities for which they care little. Nor does it help much to try to get them to face what they *ought* to do. Most people don't need their ought button pushed. That particular button has either long since been disconnected as counterproductive or it's been overworked. What they need is for someone to touch their "wanter." Sermons, half-condemning prayers, and pressure tactics are not likely to be much help here. God wants to use the challenge of our love and personal interest in others and our joy in the Lord's work to awaken others and to infect them with the life God has given us.

Furthermore, if our first concern is for people, we will spend much more time and effort finding jobs to fit people than in finding people to fit jobs, and then begging and cajoling people to help us get the work done. It's true that work needs to be done to meet human needs. But any number of jobs would be better left undone if the only way to go about it is to push and struggle to get people to do things they don't really want to do. Robert Girard, a pastor and the author of *Brethren, Hang Loose*, discovered that when he quit pushing people to do things they didn't genuinely care about, three choirs died in two months along with the midweek service and several committees. But the loss of the false, flesh-motivated life left room for a new life of the Spirit. In the long run, the loss was not a loss but a gain.

Even in the case of jobs that urgently need doing, it may be necessary first to restore the workers to spiritual health and vigor. Good work will never be done by disinterested, dispirited, overburdened workers. Such people need to be nourished, restored, and remotivated before they can be put to work. This is a concern that must be faced much more effectively than most churches seem to be able to do.

So we come back to the needs of the people we wish to serve. What are their needs? How can those needs be met? How can men and women be built up and motivated? What are the gifts God has given to each? How can those gifts best be developed and used? How can all the people be freed to become what God wants them to be and freed to use the gifts God has given them? Organization in and of itself can do nothing to meet needs of this sort. Only the outflowing life and love of God can do this. But once there is life, structures and organizations can be created to channel that life and make it more effective.

Pastoritis

The third problem that stands in the way of church renewal of the kind that concerns us here is what I call *pastoritis*. I refer to the tendency that so many churches and church members have of placing the pastor in a special position as a professional Christian or a professional worker for the church. It's the old pastor–versus–laity problem. I know very few pastors who are happy about the special way people view their position, but people everywhere seem to make this unscriptural distinction. The disease of pastoritis is pandemic.

First of all, people tend to set pastors apart as a special kind of Christian. They're supposed to have the Christian life all figured out and not have problems like other people. If they do, just listen to the tongues wag! They are not even supposed to have special friends like other people because that shows favoritism. Also, as special Christians, there should be absolutely no end to their willingness to spend themselves for others. Now it's true that Christians should so spend themselves. The fault lies in making such demands only of pastors and of no one else.

Just as damaging to the life of the church is the unshakable tendency to think of pastors as professional paid workers. Basically it is their job to keep the church going. After all, that's what we pay them for: the administrative work, visitation (of *everyone* in the church; a visit from another church member or even a church officer doesn't count), counseling, leadership in the community, youth work, secretarial and janitorial duties, and, of course, outstanding preaching. (We conveniently forget that with all the responsibilities he has, he cannot possibly find time for the prayer and study that are vital to the preparation of those outstanding sermons.) Then, of course, they should also be good family people. Ministers who neglect their families are poor testimonies to the gospel. And so the list of demands grows, on and on and on.

What's more, pastors must do all these things well else the churches are likely to go downhill. So if they have serious deficiencies in several of these areas, we really don't want them as pastors. In short, we expect them to have and exercise a variety of gifts that God almost never gives to one person. In fact, we scarcely even bother to ask what special gifts God has given them. Much less do we ask ourselves what we can do to free our pastors to devote their time to use their gifts.

The tragedy of it all is that the people in the church never fully learn to develop their own gifts. We are not a body, each member freely exercising his gifts. The pastor has to exercise them all. *Our* main job is to fill the pews, or, if we are exceptionally able or committed, to take some church office or serve on a committee. True, the church could not get along without us. True, some of the gifts do find expression. But we're not basically set up to be a body of believers, each exercising his gifts. Instead, we're an organization with a professional paid head. And, ironically, it is the gift of preaching—the one gift that every pastor has to take major responsibility for—that suffers most. The preacher has no time to do it well. At the same time, others in the congregation who have this gift are shut out from any in-depth contribution. The only way a lay person can exercise a preaching gift is in bits and pieces by pulpit supply here and there. Either that or he has to become a pastor and be saddled with a million and one other responsibilities he isn't fitted for. Is it any wonder that so little effective preaching is heard in the churches across our land?

How different is the scriptural view of the church! We are not an organization with a professional head. Christ is the head, and we, including the pastor, are His body. And in this body are hundreds of different parts, each part with its own function, and each part vital for the building up of the whole. I repeat what Paul said, "[Christ] is the head, and on him the whole body depends. Bonded and knit together by every constituent joint, the whole frame grows through the due activity of each part, and builds itself up in love" (Eph. 4:15–16 NEB). This is what the church needs to be. We are the losers when we allow the disease of pastoritis to flourish.

LIVING IN AN IMPERFECT CHURCH

Up to this point I've been dealing with some of the things that need to happen in a church before it can be transformed into a genuine fellowship of grace. This is all very well and good. But most of us still find ourselves in churches that are not very much like what they should be, and most of us are not in a position to institute significant changes. What should we do in such a situation?

One thing we dare not do is to start criticizing or pointing the finger: "Nobody ever does anything around here except to warm pews." "The pastor never gives us any solid teaching." "The church is organized all wrong."

"Nobody ever has a chance to find or use his gifts." All of these criticisms may or may not be true. But criticism seldom helps, especially if it is backed by frustration, resentment, hostility, and condemnation. The beginning point for any healing is always grace. Anyone can begin here. It does not take a total restructuring of the church to start living grace in one's church relationships. And that's where everything must start.

Another thing that we can do is to become part of a small group where grace life and fellowship are at work. We cannot change the whole church, but we can covenant with a few people to try to learn this kind of life together. A small group is the easiest place to learn, and it's almost always possible to find some small group that will meet our needs. Preferably it should be a group in some way affiliated with the church. (It's the church that needs to be changed. And how is anything going to happen there if all the most committed people pull out and find their deepest fellowship somewhere else?) But if this is impossible, there are usually other groups to be found. Either way, the group needs to be one where the members are committed to learning mutual trust, honesty, and genuine love for one another.

Yet another possibility is to break off fellowship in the church we attend and find another fellowship that more nearly meets our needs. This alternative should, however, be used only as a last resort. It too easily smacks of self-righteousness and rejection of God's people. I do not say that a time never comes to pull out and start afresh, but this should be done only under urgent need or in response to a clear, God-given opportunity. Above all, we should resist the impulse to try to find the perfect church. It does not exist. If it did, our presence would soon flaw that perfection.

Then where does the answer lie? Most of us will simply be called upon to build more grace into the church relationships and responsibilities we already have. It is astonishing how infectious and revitalizing a handful of grace-filled Christians can be. In time, as we grow in grace ourselves, the Lord may give us opportunities to act as agents of deeper healing and change in the place where God has set us.

13 | COMMUNICATING GRACE TO A WORLD IN NEED

It would be ridiculous in a book such as this to say nothing about the problem of grace in society. For one thing, one needs to ask whether it is even possible to apply the principle of accepting, uncondemning grace to the life and structure of a society necessarily predicated upon the reward of merit and the punishment of wrongdoing. If it is possible, how can it be done?

The central problem in applying grace within the larger framework of society is similar to that in applying grace to children in the home. How does one convey grace without undercutting the claims of righteousness and justice? Both grace and justice are necessary. How does one combine them?

One might be tempted to think that in a necessarily impersonal society based on law, grace would be a luxury too expensive even to contemplate. After all, people have to get what they deserve. If a person wants the necessities of life, he should work for them. If he commits a crime, he should be punished. But how shall we deal with the criminal without confirming him in his crime and making him even worse? I contend, therefore, that grace is at least a part of the answer.

It takes little perception to see that not much grace is at work in society as it now exists. As a society, we do not accept people as they are. Much less do we manifest the grace that gives the kind of unconditional acceptance that reaches out to meet human need wherever it is found. Rather, we live in a turmoil of prejudice and condemnation of one another. Conventional people despise the counterculture as sexually loose, weird, irresponsible—even unclean. Races resent other races, looking down their noses at those who are "different." The unconventionals for their part condemn the rest of us with at least equal vigor. They detest us for our racism, our materialism, our oppression of the poor, our rape of the environment, our economic imperialism.

It's not that either side is blameless. Far from it! But that's the point. Each of us has enough sin, enough selfishness, to keep us fully occupied correcting our own misdeeds without spending time and energy pointing the finger at one another. Instead, we destroy one another with our self-righteous condemnation and rejection of each other. Human beings for whom Christ died become less than dirt in our eyes. Those on the other side of the fence are not even worth listening to. Much less are they worth helping. We almost feel that if they would go away and leave us alone— or perhaps go to live in a foreign country—we'd all be better off. The net result is that by our very attitude, by our non-grace, by our rejection of one another we make impossible the very kind of change that we feel is needed. We alienate one another and then wonder why more love and responsibility are not to be found.

What we need is a new infusion of the grace of God into our relationships—the grace that made Jesus come, not to call the righteous but sinners; the grace that led Jesus to die for us while we were yet sinners. The world needs again to see grace incarnate, embodied in personal action. As God's grace once had to be demonstrated in the person of the living, loving Christ, it now must be demonstrated by living, loving people who have been touched by the grace of Christ and are committed to sharing it.

But the grace that we manifest cannot be simply a shapeless benevolence any more than the grace of Christ was. It needs to be a grace, an acceptance, that is vibrant with the passion for justice. It cannot say, "I accept you as you are and value you as a person for whom Christ died, but I don't care how much you abuse your neighbor or how much he abuses you or how much of a blackguard or misanthrope you both become." In fact, precisely because grace values each individual regardless of who he is or what he's done it will not settle for the betrayal of human value that lies behind all selfishness, all sin, all oppression. In short, grace will always insist, and insist very loudly, upon the need for justice in human affairs.

So the question remains. How does one demonstrate the acceptance of grace and at the same time do justice to the demands of morality, responsibility, and fair dealing in society? Or, to put it another way, how does one love the sinner and at the same time hate the sin and deal effectively with it?

Again (as in the case of children in the home) we must have recourse to rules or laws and their consistent, even-handed enforcement. In other words, each individual has to be made to face the consequences of his own selfishness and lawlessness. No sinner or criminal is ever helped by a treatment that saves him the trouble of coming to grips with his own destructive behavior and attitudes. So all destructive behavior must have its specified consequence or penalty.

There is nothing new about this. The world has never known a large heterogeneous society that could get along without laws and law enforcement. It never will. My point is that grace can and must coexist with this structure of laws. We have to administer these laws without personal attitudes of rancor, condemnation, rejection, self-righteousness. We must see that lawless behavior, insofar as possible, always gets its due, but at the same time that the offender is not spurned, devalued, dehumanized in the process. There has to be a concern for the lawbreaker as a person, even when we have to punish him.

In saying this, I am painfully aware that I am just talking theory. And I'm afraid that's about all I can do. It's up to all of us to put the theory into practice, especially the politicians, judges, jailers, lawyers, and police officers. If there's going to be any grace in our society, every one of us must begin treating others—whatever their background—with acceptance and outgoing love.

By the same token, we will never know grace in our society unless its members—many of them—learn the power of grace in their own lives. We need men and women who are able to face their own failures, inadequacies, and selfishness without dishonesty and without continual breast-beating. We need those who, by actual experience, know what it is to love sinners and yet detest their sin. This is grace.

We need men and women, too, who care not only about the miseries of the individual human beings whom they meet, but about the miseries of human beings in the mass—miseries and injustices that come about through inadequacies and injustice in the system as a whole. I think, for example, of the deplorable situation in our prisons. It's all very well to say that the inmates have asked for it, but that fact neither excuses the dehumanization that takes place nor does it solve the problem. When I see what our penal system is like, I'm almost tempted to think that if we had wanted to construct a system that destroys and corrupts human beings and creates criminals, we could hardly have dreamed up anything more effective than our present way of dealing with lawbreakers. We take a person away from spouse and family, shut him up with hostile, cynical, embittered prisoners, and leave him there in his own specially prepared hell. We turn him loose again in the society that so degraded him and then wonder why we have problems with law and order.

Prisons are by no means our only problem—or even the worst one. What shall we say about poverty, unemployment, economic oppression, child and spouse abuse, abortion, racial discrimination, drug addiction, alcoholism, neglect of the aged, and a host of other evils? There will never be easy answers to these problems. But Christians must be concerned about them, and Christians must give leadership in thinking through workable solutions and putting them into effect. Such concern and leadership have made major contributions to meeting human needs in the past and they must do so again. Even if it means personal labor and sacrifice; even if it means major changes in our comfortable, secure system and way of life, we must commit ourselves as a company of grace-filled men and women to share the grace of Christ in a society aching with need.

If we are thus concerned for the needs and hurts of human beings in this confused and struggling society of ours, we will find that our spoken message about the grace of God in Christ will go forth with new, life-changing power. Men and women will listen to us as they once listened to the loving, serving Christ long ago.

What's more, we ourselves will not shrink to tell men and women about this message of grace that God has committed to us, this message that changes human hearts and teaches them to love one another. As God enables us, we will share it personally with friends and acquaintances. Individually and corporately we will broadcast it to those who have never heard. In season and out of season, we will seek to preach the Good News of redemption, the news that God loves sinners, the news that "God was reconciling the world to himself in Christ, not counting men's sins against them." We will beseech men "on Christ's behalf" to be "reconciled to God" (2 Cor. 5:19–20). This is the imperative that God's grace lays upon us.

14 | CONCLUSION: GROWING IN GRACE

Once after I had preached a sermon on grace, a woman who had heard me remarked to a friend of mine, "I didn't need that message." That reaction, I confess, left me wondering what to think. I can only hope that Christian readers will not feel the same way about this book, for if anyone has been able to read this far without realizing his need for a deeper experience of grace, I shall have failed—at least for that particular reader. Grace is not the kind of thing that you can study once or experience once, and then conclude that you have it nailed down. You can never conclude that you've learned what needs to be learned, and that nothing more needs to be said or done. There's always more to learn, more to understand, more to appropriate, more to be lived. Grace needs to permeate deeper and deeper and deeper into our minds, attitudes, feelings, relationships, behavior, service for God and others. It needs to go on and on changing us. It needs to become an ever more vital, motivating force in our lives. There's no end to the learning and growing we need to do.

The apostle gets right to the heart of it all when he tells us to "grow in the grace and knowledge of our Lord and Savior Jesus Christ" (2 Peter 3:18). We all need to grow in grace. There's not a Christian anywhere who doesn't need to. There is simply no alternative. Whether we like it or not, whether we are aware of it or not, we must grow in this area of our lives.

And we need at least three things if we are to grow in grace: We must expose ourselves to grace; we must appropriate it; and we must express it. Furthermore, we need to do these things continually. Not once. Not twice. But over and over and over again, every day of our lives.

EXPOSURE TO GRACE

If we are to learn more of the transforming power of grace, we must expose ourselves to it, to its message and influence. This exposure is going to mean, first and foremost, a continuing and ever-growing exposure to the grace of Christ Himself. He is the prime demonstration of the grace of God. In Him, the grace of God is fully incarnate. If we look at Him, we will see, as John did, that the glory of the Father rests upon Him, "full of grace and truth" (1:14).

Again and again we need to remember the grace of our Lord, who "though he was rich, yet for your sakes . . . became poor, so that you through his poverty might become rich" (2 Cor. 8:9). We need to see His gracious way with sinners, with Zacchaeus, with the woman taken in adultery, with those who crucified Him. We need to see how willingly He gave Himself to people to serve them by His life and to redeem them by His death. We need to saturate our minds and hearts in the wonder of what He did and what He was and is. We need to realize more and more "the breadth and length and height and depth of the love of Christ, and to know it, though it is beyond knowledge" so that we may "attain to fullness of being, the fullness of God himself" (Eph. 3:18–19 NEB).

Exposure to grace means not only exposure to the grace of Christ, but also exposure to scriptural teachings on the subject of grace. It means reading and rereading the classic passages dealing with the subject: especially Galatians, Romans 1–8, and Ephesians 2. It means knowing those passages backward and forward, understanding the line of argument, being able to think one's way through them, immersing oneself in the truth of them, even memorizing them. It also means searching through the Scriptures for teaching on the subject. It means learning to understand God's whole plan in the light of the grace of God that lies behind it.

Let me add one suggestion, however. When we read the Scriptures, we should do so with our grace spectacles on. I say this not to urge people to twist Scripture to make it say something it doesn't say. (No one has the right to do that with any book, much less with the written Word of God.) I say it, rather, to counteract the very human tendency to want to read Scripture under the false light of legalism. At one time, I was scarcely able to read a single word in the Bible without writhing under a sense of guilt, failure, and condemnation. I wanted to love God and obey Him, but every commandment in Scripture left me climbing the walls. Even such a simple verse as John 14:15 destroyed me: "If you love me, you will obey what I command." I couldn't help but read it almost as if it said, "Earn my love by keeping my commandments." I felt as if I were not and could not keep Christ's commandments, and therefore was cut off from a relationship with Him.

Because of the terrible price that accompanied defectiveness, I couldn't face the fact that my love was defective. I couldn't see that if I didn't love Christ, no amount of effort to keep His commandments would ever prove a thing, but that if I did love Him, I would *want* to keep them. When you love someone you express it. So when we love Christ we must and will express our love by obeying Him. There's no legalism in that. It's simple truth. That's how love will and must work.

Thus when we read our Bibles, we should *assume* the grace of God. If we do, everything we read will look different. When I first began to see the teachings of Scripture in this new light, everything was transformed. I still believed the old basics of the faith. They were still what I had always believed. But now they looked totally different. One doctrine in Scripture after another sprang to vibrant life and meaning. They became exciting to me in a way they never had been before. Grace had entered the picture, and nothing would ever be the same again.

Finally, we need to expose ourselves to grace not only in Christ and the Scriptures, but through our relationships with other Christians. Whether we like it or not, none of us can sustain a growing experience of the grace of God on a strictly private relationship with Him. It's true that we all must have a vital, personal, private relationship with God, but the Scriptures know nothing about a Christian experience that stops there. Grace has to come to us not only at the hand of God but at the hand of others also. Or, to put it another way, other people are the means God uses to convey His grace to us.

In fact, if we are in a situation where no one really knows us or loves us just as we are or reaches out to give of himself to meet our needs, it is almost impossible to find much meaning in the idea of God's acceptance. The grace is all theoretical—off in the fantasy world of wish fulfillment or empty intellectualization. But the legalism, the non-grace, the sense of worthlessness and rejection are real. They are what we experience and live with every day. It's hard to rest in God's uncondemning love and acceptance if we feel that the people around us are ignoring us, condemning us, criticizing us, putting us down. If grace is to mean anything to us, it has to have feet that run to meet us, hands that reach out to us, eyes that see us, a mouth that speaks to us, a heart that loves us and cares what happens to us. That is why Jesus had to become part of the human race. That is why, when Jesus left us. He handed His task on to the church. That is why the Holy Spirit is given to each individual believer—so that we may be filled with grace and minister that grace to one another.

Grace comes to us in any number of ways at the hands of others. Ideally, however, we all need this human touch of grace in at least four kinds of relationships. If we are lacking in any of these areas, we will sooner or later suffer from the lack. These four areas comprise relationships with a family or living group, with close friends or confidants, with small fellowship groups, and with a church congregation.

The importance of exposure to grace in the family relationship needs no further comment, for the need is so obvious and the effects of the pressure or absence of grace here are so far-reaching. Almost equally obvious is the importance of grace in the church. However, again I emphasize the fact that both small and large groups are needed. Only in small groups can Christians get to know one another in depth, come to accept each other in more than a superficial way, and learn to be open, honest, and giving. But only in a larger group or congregation (if it is functioning properly) can one find a solid teaching and preaching ministry, a widening of horizons with many different kinds of Christians and a pooling of resources (time, money, skills, organization) to meet larger areas of human need. The smaller group infects the large by the vitality of its life and meaning. The large group serves the small with its greater resources and lifts it beyond itself.

But close friends are also necessary. When problems arise in the family, other family members are too caught up in the situation to provide necessary help and counsel. The church as a whole is too large and impersonal. The small group? Well, there are some things you simply don't feel free to share with them. They might not understand. But a friend who understands, who listens, who accepts, who cares? That relationship is beyond price. We all of us need at least one friend with whom we can be wholly ourselves, wholly honest, wholly accepted. It's a great sorrow that for many of us this need goes essentially unmet.

These, then, are the four types of relationships that all of us need. Alas! Too few of us are finding grace at all four of these levels. Some of us (God forgive us all!) are hard put to find grace anywhere at all. If you are in this situation, I can only urge you not to lash out at your plight or condemn your family, acquaintances, the church you attend. Instead, start praying and looking around. Ask God to lead you to at least one friend who accepts you and cares about you, and whom you can trust. However, a price is to be paid to establish a relationship with such a friend. If we want to know the renewing power of his acceptance and grace, we have to be willing to open up. We have to share our problems, our needs, our feelings, our hopes, and our fears.

It means nothing to be accepted just as we are if we make sure that no one ever finds out who we are or what we are like. So there is a risk here. But the risk is worth taking to experience the grace of God in our relationships.

APPROPRIATING GOD'S GRACE

If we are to learn the grace life, we need not only to be exposed to it continually, but we need to appropriate God's grace. All the exposure in the world is not going to help us unless day by day we open our hearts to that grace and make it our own.

Recognize our need

If we are going to appropriate God's grace, we first of all have continually to recognize our need. Some people never appropriate the grace of God because they never really see the need. They are reasonably satisfied with life. When they have problems, they are able to cope with them. And they feel no great need for forgiveness. Misunderstanding the nature of sin and their alienation from God, they feel that they've never done anything all that bad. So what if God is gracious? What's that got to do with them? They don't need it. So they don't reach out and take it.

Others have accepted grace as a sort of article of faith, but it never really means much to them. They more or less take it for granted. Of *course* God is gracious. Why wouldn't He be? Who didn't know that? Why, they accepted Christ years ago, and their sins were washed away. And that was that! Nor can they understand how we get so emotional over God's unconditional acceptance. Now, for the prostitute or the drug addict or the derelict on skid row, grace might be a different matter. Those down-and-outs really need to change. It does them good to meet the grace of God, get saved, and start leading responsible, productive lives. But the rest of us? What's all the fuss about? We don't happen to need that message.

Both groups of people—those who see no need of grace at all or those who take it for granted—must experience a deep-down recognition of personal need. They need to face the law of God in all its purity and beauty and recognize the huge performance gap between what God's perfect law of love requires and what they themselves actually do. It may take some deep personal tragedy or some experience of utter failure before such people can see their need. But see it they must.

Others of us shy away in a different way from recognizing our need. We know very well that we fall short, but we simply cannot accept the fact. It rankles deep down within our hearts and never allows us a moment of rest. One would almost think that we were determined to have no heartsease until we reach the place where we no longer need grace—as if God came to call only the righteous, not sinners in need of a Savior.

The fact is that we must recognize our permanent need. The richest Christian is not the one who has matured so that he no longer needs grace. He is the one who has accepted, once and for all, his own moral indigence, and has learned ceaselessly to open his heart to the never-ending flow of grace from the Father's hand. Only those who are continually aware of their need can continually appropriate the bounty of divine grace and be changed thereby.

Confess our sins

If we are going to appropriate grace in our lives, we need not only to acknowledge our general need, but also to deal with our particular failures. We must be ready to repent of known sin and to confess it. Nothing so effectively gets in the way of the operation of grace as unrepented, unconfessed sin. "If we confess our sins," John tells us, God is "faithful and just and will forgive us our sins and purify us from all unrighteousness" (1 John 1:9).

I want to make it clear that confession is not something God needs before He can humble Himself to have a relationship with us. Nor is His demand for confession a legalistic one. Confession is not the pound of flesh that He exacts from us before He is willing to be nice. God is not the kind of Person who freezes us out as a punishment for our misdeeds or as a means of compelling submission. The problem is not any need or arbitrary requirement on God's part. Our need for confession arises out of the necessity to see sin for what it is and repent of it.

Suppose, for example, you had been my friend for many years, and then I turned around and began to spread all kinds of vicious lies about you. Then suppose I came to you as if nothing had happened and expected you to resume the friendship. (After all, you shouldn't get on your high horse about it all. You should accept me as I am.) Could we then have any kind of true relationship? Even if you could forgive me, my behavior would stand in the way. It would signal loudly and clearly that our friendship was meaningless to me, and that I had no real respect for you. If you, for your part, could remove all barriers between us, my own wall of indifference, dishonesty, and selfishness would still be there. For me, there would still be no truth in the relationship, no love, no redemptive and revitalizing power.

It all boils down to this: If I have allowed selfishness to mar a relationship, there is no renewal, no truth for me unless I face what I have done, realize the depth of the hurt, and feel genuinely sorry for my wrongdoing. And if I am sorry for what I've done, I need to say so, not only for the sake of the one I have wronged, but also for my own. As long as I hold back from open confession, just so long do I refrain from full honesty and full commitment to the one I have sinned against. In fact, if I am truly sorry, I will *want* to say so.

There's no getting around the necessity for confession. Unconfessed sin destroys relationships, if not on the part of the one wronged, then always and inevitably on the part of the one doing the wrong. It's impossible to enjoy forgiveness or redemptive renewal if one has done a wrong that he refuses to confess.

Furthermore, the confession (if it is to be redemptive) must be genuine. That is, it cannot be done merely as a duty. It cannot be forced. It cannot be extracted or exhorted. It must be free and from the heart. In fact, it is doubtful whether there are many deep, grace-filled relationships either between people or between people and God, that have not been cemented together by just such redemptive experiences. Sin, repentance, confession, forgiveness. These are the things that build honesty, truth, acceptance, trust. Would to God we were humble enough to do it more often.

When I say, however, that we need more experiences of genuine confession, I do not mean to suggest that there should be the kind of sensitivity to wrongdoing that stifles the spirit—the kind that leaves one almost afraid to breathe for fear of doing something wrong. This attitude does not come from grace, for grace not only forgives—it also forbears. In any relationship lurk a thousand little imperfections that love covers. Falsehood at the heart? Never! There must always be a full accounting of such attitudes or behavior. But the countless little things? Love just passes them by. If they are symptoms of something more important, they will be dealt with in their time.

God has this same spirit of patient forbearance with our spiritual infirmities. He understands our failures. He knows what it is going to take to deal with them when the time comes. I suspect, in fact, that God seldom deals with more than one thing at a time in our lives. He is infinitely patient, and He knows just when and how to work with each aspect that requires change, repentance, or confession. Meantime, love covers. This also is grace.

Constantly reaffirm God's grace

If we are truly to appropriate God's grace, we need not only to acknowledge our need of grace and confess our sins, but also continually to reaffirm that grace. It's so easy to slip back into the old non-grace patterns of earning God's pleasure and feeling that He has rejected us when we fail. We need to keep on coming back and back and back to the fundamental fact of God's unconditional love and forgiveness. When we find ourselves feeling negative toward God, we need to remind ourselves that God is not what we imagine Him to be. No matter what we feel or think, God is always kinder, greater, better, more beautiful than we ever could have thought. Even in our very wildest dreams, we have no conception of how good He is. Even His severity toward us is goodness. By no means could we have something more or better than we already have in Him.

Again, when we find ourselves feeling negative toward ourselves, we need to remember that "even this God loves." It is sinners He cares about. It's sinners Jesus died for. It does not matter how nasty or out of sorts we feel or how frustrated, how discouraged, how far from God. "For I am convinced that there is nothing in death or life, in the realm of spirits or superhuman powers, in the world as it is or the world as it shall be, in the forces of the universe, in heights or depths—nothing in all creation that can separate us from the love of God in Christ Jesus our Lord" (Rom. 8:38–39 NEB).

Live in conscious fellowship with God

In the final analysis, appropriating God's grace simply means maintaining a continual, conscious fellowship with God. It means being aware of His loving presence; it means listening to Him as He speaks to us through the pages of Scripture, through the voice of His Spirit in our hearts, and through the words and deeds of the people He sends to us. It means talking to Him as a kind or sometimes a stern Father or as an understanding Friend. It means loving Him, obeying Him, serving Him. It means sharing His passion for suffering humanity. It means learning to know His will and doing it. Only so can the grace of God become a living, life-changing reality in our lives.

EXPRESSING THE GRACE OF GOD

Here we come to what is perhaps the most demanding task of all: expressing the grace of God in word or deed, sharing it with others, passing it on. Here we come to the proof of all the things we say we believe, the point where the reality of our faith is put to the test. Do we care enough about the grace of God that we want to tell others about it? Has it made enough difference in our hearts that it shows in the way we live and in the way we touch the people God sends our way? Is it finding vital expression in the way we act and the way we talk?

If it is, grace will more and more express itself in all our relationships. It will show in the way we treat our friends. It will reveal itself in our church responsibilities and contacts. It will be seen in our concern for our neighbors and for the hurts of men and women everywhere.

If the grace of God has truly touched our lives, we will accept people as they are. There will be no condemning, rejecting, putting people down; no self-righteous superiority; no how-could-yous. And we will forgive. Not once, not twice, not seven times, but seventy times seven. And we will give: our encouragement, our witness, our money, our concern, our time, our love, our very selves. We will give without reward, without stint, and beyond desert. As our Lord gave Himself for us, so we will give ourselves for others. Freely we have received. Freely we must give.

God grant that His grace may keep on penetrating deeper and deeper and deeper so that this grace may be expressed ever more fully in our lives. May He teach us always to "grow in the grace and knowledge of our Lord and Savior Jesus Christ."

> Now I commit you to God and to the word of his grace, which can build you up and give you an inheritance among all those who are sanctified (Acts 20:32).